WALKING THE WALK

SPIRITUAL PRINCIPLES
IN THE EPISTLE OF JAMES

Walking the Walk

Spiritual Principles in the Epistle of James

Alan Jefferies

The Pentland Press Limited
Edinburgh · Cambridge · Durham · USA

Scripture taken from the Holy Bible,
New International Version.
Copyright © 1973, 1978, 1984
by International Bible Society.
Used by permission of
Hodder and Stoughton Limited.

First published in 2001 by
The Pentland Press Ltd.
1 Hutton Close
South Church
Bishop Auckland
Durham

British Library Cataloguing in Publication Data.
A catalogue record for this book is available
from the British Library.

ISBN 1 85821 831 4

Typeset by George Wishart & Associates, Whitley Bay.
Printed and bound by Antony Rowe Ltd., Chippenham.

Acknowledgements

I owe a great debt of gratitude to the innumerable host of godly men and women whose lives and ministries have been a positive influence upon my life. What is set out in this book is in no small part due to their faithfulness. To those and especially to my wife and family I say a special thank you for your example and encouragement in spiritual matters. To be surrounded by such people is to know the favour of God.

While to mention some by name is to risk offending others, I must single out Joyce and Alan Humphries, whose help in proof-reading and encouragement in serving Jesus, makes them more than worthy of mention.

My greatest regret is that to the many who have been an influential part of my life, but have since passed on to Glory, I cannot say thank you, nor can I share this book with them. Though in heaven, their testimony still speaks.

To the One who loved me and gave Himself for me, thank You!

Contents

Introduction

It is an undeniable Christian truth that the message of Jesus Christ, like its originator, is the same yesterday, today and will continue to be so forever. Yet, central to all that Jesus taught is a theme that is often either overlooked or ignored. It is a theme that, though simple, is a vital key in unlocking power within the believer. The message of Jesus Christ is intensely practical, and works. It is not a theory or a proposal, but a real and verifiable way of living.

We should at the outset of this book note an important difference between a way of life and a way of living. What we term a 'way of life' has come to be a passive acceptance of the way our life and circumstances shape us. While when we speak of a 'way of living', we are defining an aggressive attitude that is not shaped, but itself shapes the circumstances in which our lives are conducted, and determines our destiny.

It is this aggressive lifestyle that Jesus taught during His earthly ministry, and so instilled into His disciples, that is unmistakably present in their teaching and writings. Aggressive, not to the people whose lives it touches upon, but in the way it determines to settle only for the best God has for it.

Two ingredients go into such a lifestyle. The first finds its origin in heaven, the other on the earth. The former is the power of God's Spirit, leading, guiding and strengthening. The latter is our understanding of God's Word, coupled with a desire to put that understanding into practice.

That we should do so is a vital part of our responsibility before God. Vital, for not to do so has severe effects, including a weak testimony and a powerless life. When we live in such a manner we misrepresent the very truth and nature of the Gospel message.

The believer who bears much fruit, is the believer who has grasped the need to be determined and disciplined in the way that he lives out in his day to day affairs, the powerful message of a practical Christianity. The generation in which we live will not be won to Jesus by a code of morals or a statement of beliefs. It will be won by those who live, not by what they teach, but by what Jesus taught them. The harvest fields will not be reaped by talkers but by workers. The former may abound; the latter are much rarer.

Of all the writers in the New Testament, James is the one who emphasizes the practical nature of faith. If faith is alive it will show itself in a real, visible and practical way. James views this as being at the very core of Christianity. As a result of his view there is much in his teaching that can challenge us, guide us and prepare us for Christian living. The challenge to all of us is to demonstrate a living faith, not by merely hearing the Word, or even talking about it, but by living it. As God watches our generation, will He see us talk the talk or walk the walk?

The purpose of this book is to highlight those important areas that cause us to fall short in our walk, to equip us for a harvest on earth, and our eventual destiny, a crown of glory in heaven.

While each chapter has a phrase or section from the epistle highlighting its subject, the whole epistle should be read between each chapter; no subject can be interpreted correctly or fully by a verse or section taken in isolation.

The illustrations used, where possible have been checked and confirmed to be true. Others are given as they were related to me, and are recalled as truthfully as I can. Nothing included is knowingly inaccurate.

May God bless each one of us as we endeavour to walk before Him in the way James has instructed us.

CHAPTER ONE

The Truth About Trials

Consider it pure joy, my brothers, whenever you face trials
of many kinds, because you know . . . (James 1:2-3).

Most people accept that when it comes to learning to swim there are two options. Start at the shallow end or start at the deep end. Here James starts his epistle to Jewish Christians at the deep end. He doesn't waste his time or theirs with trivialities. He starts with one of the big issues they faced in their day to day living.

We must understand too, that he is not writing to people who are thinking of embracing the Christian message, but to people who are already Christians. He is setting out what amounts to a manual to instruct, help and equip men and women like you and I to cope with the realities of life. Hence he begins his epistle by dealing with one of the most important, but probably least understood aspects of a believer's life. One of the greatest challenges any of us face when it comes to living out our Christianity, is how we act or react during times of trial. Our theology may be faultless, our knowledge of Christianity without equal, but what happens when difficulties arise is one of the benchmarks of our true spirituality. As we seek perfection, we must seek it, not through what we believe, but through the putting of such beliefs into practice.

As for trials, we all have them, but do we understand them? Do we realize that they are very much a part of the life that God has chosen for us?

For many teenagers, exams are a major part of their life, and during my teens I was no different. In the beginning I feared them, resenting two particular problems that they presented. The first was that I much preferred other things to studying, and that never changed throughout school or college, but the second did. I saw them as an opportunity to fail. I felt a pressure of personal expectation and feared failure. As I matured I understood that exams were not my enemy, they were my friend. If I wanted to go to university I needed to pass exams. I couldn't get there without them. Failing them was no worse than not sitting them. To achieve my ambitions and to realize my goals, I could not avoid having to sit them. If I passed them, the end result would bring greater joy than the pain encountered along the way.

I was never the brightest pupil, but coming to terms with exams helped me. I often performed better in exams than others who throughout the year had shown more intelligence and had worked harder. The reason was that I understood that exams were not there to break me, but to make me. They would also help me in later life to understand an important spiritual principle. I could hate the idea of exams; I could fear them; or I could accept that if I mastered them, they would take me where I wanted to go and help me to become what I wanted to be. Trials are no different.

If the student undergoes trial by exam, the Christian undergoes examination by trial. Men and women of God are not special because they avoid trials, but because of what happens during them. Trials, if we understand them, will take us as believers into a new and fresh revelation of God. They will help make us into what we ought to be.

When it comes to understanding trials, James can speak with great authority. It is believed that the James who wrote this epistle was the half-brother of the Lord Jesus Christ, and one of the early Christian leaders in Jerusalem. As such, it is certain that he would have known great persecution and the obvious trials that accompanied such opposition. There were few places in the early days of the Church that knew the intensity of opposition that the believers in Jerusalem faced. The Acts of the Apostles paints a vivid picture of the trials that believers such as James underwent. His epistle may well have been motivated by concern for those who fled Jerusalem for other parts of the Roman Empire, in order to safeguard their lives.

Not only did James live in such difficult and perilous times, but according to tradition he would go on to die a martyr's death. He is more than adequately qualified to speak from experience on the subject of trials.

That he understood their importance is clear, but what is also evident is that he felt we all needed to understand them. Unless we first understand the importance and role of trials, we will never understand the role of God in our lives, or our role in His service.

Trials are part of our lives. Among many that may not hold Christian beliefs, there is a view that Christianity represents a form of escapism from the harsh realities of life. Little could be further from the truth.

James does not suggest how we should react if we encounter trials, or what we should do if, through disobedience, we find ourselves in difficulties. He tells us that we will have trials to experience. The addict cannot break his addiction until he understands that he is addicted, and the Christian cannot know victory in trials until he understands why he must encounter them.

Some Christians live and teach the view that difficulty and problem circumstances only arise as a result of disobedience. To believe such a view is unbiblical, and to live it is to live a lie. It is as a result of such beliefs that some falter and others turn back in their pursuit of holiness.

Of course disobedience brings its own rewards. Israel and

Judah throughout the Old Testament brought needless suffering on themselves through obvious disobedience and unfaithfulness to God. That, however, is not the context in which James is writing.

Jesus taught His disciples in John 15 that they would know tribulation, persecution and opposition. This was conditional on one thing; that they were following Him. As long as they were His disciples, they would have problems. They were not to feel guilty or ashamed. They were not to pretend that they were too spiritual to have problems. They were to face them, accept them as part of their lives and treat them accordingly. For some people, opposition may well be proof that they are living in the plan and purpose of God and not the contrary.

This being the case, how we react at such times is a great test of the validity of our spiritual understanding. What one man perceives to be punishment may well be viewed by another as preparation.

The follower of Jesus belongs to a kingdom that, though it exists in this world, is not a part of it. The powers of evil are constantly warring against that kingdom for control of a world that is destined for Christ's eternal rule. Such is the battle that is taking place, that Paul writes in 2 Timothy 3:12 warning his young friend Timothy to expect persecution, and therefore opposition and trials, as he seeks to live a life that is pleasing to God.

Trials do not prove that God has given us up as a bad job. It is more likely to be the case that He is busy making a better job of us than is already the case. When we understand this truth we are on the way to understanding the purpose of trials and how to treat them.

I remember being reminded that the only people who lived in constant sunshine were those who lived in the desert, devoid of all the beauty that rain showers bring to the garden. It is often the experiences we would choose not to encounter, that, like rain, produce fruit and prevent the bareness of the desert in our lives.

James was not embarrassed by hardship. He counted it as joy. This was because he understood what was happening. He knew it was not punishment. He understood that the purpose of God in allowing such things to come into his life was for his own benefit. He wasn't the only man in the Bible to understand this principle.

Paul wrote in Romans 8:28-29 that God takes all that comes our way and turns it to our good, whatever the motivation behind it. He uses such trials to shape our lives in the image of Jesus. This is at the very centre of understanding trials.

Joseph understood way back in the Old Testament (Genesis 50) about this principle. Having been misrepresented, beaten, mocked, sold into slavery and lied about by his own brothers, he did not seek revenge. He treated them mercifully; not because he failed to understand their motives, but because he understood that though their motivation was evil, God had allowed what had happened to take place. Whatever the motives of others, God was in overall control of every situation that befell him, and looking to both bless Joseph and make him a blessing to others.

If being like Jesus is the greatest motivating factor of our lives, trials become opportunities and not problems. What others intend as evil, we will see God turn into good. There are two words that sound similar in the English language, but have two distinct and different meanings. These two words are very important in understanding truth. The words are perception and deception. We must be careful that what we perceive does not deceive. The spirit of the age is ease. Yet what we perceive as good can deceive us and be bad. A job that has tough deadlines may be difficult, but it may be the chisel that God uses to sculpt you in the image of Jesus. The hostile environment in which you live may at times feel desperately unpleasant, but it may be what is needed to make you as clay in the hands of the Potter. What you perceive to be bad may cause you to be deceived into making the wrong decisions. What may appear as problems may be opportunities to be light in darkness.

Jesus was not deceived by perception because He understood how God could take evil motives and show His glory. In John 8 we read an account of a woman who had been trapped in an adulterous relationship. Those who had caught her now sought to trap Jesus. He knew their motives, but He also knew God's. The account tells us something of the love, mercy, compassion and forgiveness of God. Jesus wasn't threatened by the pressure that others sought to place Him under, or the evil motives of men, because He knew God has His own agenda.

Once we understand that God's agenda in our lives is to shape us and mould us, we are not frightened by trials. We can welcome them as friends, not fear them as enemies. God uses what may be perceived as unwelcome intrusions into our lives to strengthen us, to develop us, to teach us, and even to prune us as a gardener does his plants. Whatever and however, it is always for our good.

Though we can only be what God wants us to be when we allow Him to shape us through the experiences of life, this is not the full picture. We can only be what He wants us to be when we experience first hand His power and deliverance.

Some believers understand the need of trials to be a part of their life, but do not understand that defeat is most certainly not a part. God is compassionate by nature. He does not inflict suffering to pressurize us for the sake of it. God desires that we know trials to help us, not to depress us, disappoint us or defeat us. If we are to be like Jesus, we will have to know victory over circumstances and trials. Living like Jesus is living in victory.

Every prize worth claiming, every medal worth wearing, every war worth winning was done so at a cost. The cost was the overcoming of that which stood in the way of victory. Trials may come in all shapes and sizes, but victory only comes in one. Overcoming!

Often top sportsmen and sportswomen attempt to stay at the top longer than perhaps they should. Maybe they attempt one race, one match or one fight too many. Why? The answer is to be found in the taste of victory. It's more than the additional achievement; it's not the need to prove something more to themselves. With all that has already been achieved, why carry on the hardships of training and preparation? It's the taste of triumph. It's the taste of overcoming. It's the taste of staring trials in the face and overcoming them.

As Christians we should not underestimate the experience of victory over trials. The taste is good. David encourages us in Psalm 34:8 that we should taste and see the goodness of God. He is exhorting us to taste God's victorious power over the trials we face. Not having to concede defeat in times of difficulty. To still be standing while others are weak at the knees; to be at peace while others are in turmoil; to have hope while others only have dismay. All this should cause us to rejoice, not in the plight of others, but in the goodness of God in taking our side and giving us the taste of victory. It's a taste that we can come to enjoy. It's a taste that's not available in bottles, only in trials.

There is still one other key element in the purpose of trials that we must consider. In James 1:12 we read of the reward that comes to those who triumph in adversity. There is the 'crown of life' that the victorious believer will receive from his God.

To the first century believer the idea of a crown conjured up the idea of joy, rejoicing, celebration and victory. For the man whose love for God causes him not to give up or turn his back on God during difficult times, a great reward awaits. A celebration of joy, of rejoicing and of life itself awaits him. Life is enriched by victory itself, but even more so, by the blessing of God.

We must not forget that our pilgrimage on earth is the start of the journey, not the end of the road. Jesus advises us all alike to consider the need to be storing up treasure, not in the bank or building society, but in heaven. Where better to be sowing seed that reaps eternal reward than in obedience and faithfulness in time of trial? Such investment reaps great reward.

James also points out another important principle about trials. They are diverse. What is a trial to one may not be to another. The trial or trials that are relevant to my life are personal and cannot be judged rightly by another person; nor can they be assessed by another's attitude to them. They cannot even be measured or evaluated by others who may have been in similar circumstances. They are personal, between God and myself.

One believer may face trials with regard to finance. Obedience in giving and trusting God to stretch what remains into enough, is for some a great trial. Coping with bereavement or loneliness may be a greater trial for others. The issue is not the nature of trials, but the certainty and diversity of them. No two trials are the same, just as no two people are the same.

In understanding this, we must be careful that we do not make the mistake of being wrongly influenced by other people and their experiences. A situation may arise within your walk with God that appears to be minor or insignificant to another. Their advice may well belittle the trial you find yourself undergoing, but for you it may be the turning point in your destiny. It may affect you and others around you to a greater extent than any man on earth knows. Accordingly you must treat it with the utmost seriousness.

How every one of us reacts in such circumstances will be a determining factor to the outcome of our destiny. Our lives are often shaped, and our destiny determined by things that may go unnoticed by others. It is certain though that our destiny will not be reached if such things go unnoticed by us. Every event that comes into our life is significant enough for God to know about it, permit it and use it for our good.

The devil will seek to expose those areas of our lives that are weak and outside of God's control; those areas that we have not surrendered to His Lordship. If he fails in one area, he will look in another. Similarly God, who seeks to prove us and lead us to victory, seeks to do so in every area of our lives. Therefore it should not surprise us that trials are diverse in nature.

However different or diverse the circumstance may be, the answer is always the same. We seek to apply the principles we read in the Bible. We grasp the truth, that when life leads us into a valley, it is that God may lead us out the other side. The trials we face may be emotional, financial, medical, psychological or sexual, but irrespective of the source of the circumstances, the answer is not found in circumstance, it is found in God's Spirit applying God's Word to our lives.

We must allow God to guide us, but we must exercise perseverance ourselves. James 1:12 lays down a key to trials. It is not those who start out, but those who endure to the end that find reward from God. Church history may be littered with those who started well but fainted, but it has clearly been shaped by those who finished well, irrespective of their start. Gold medals are not given to the first to start, but to the first to finish.

One such man to finish well is Abraham. He started out well enough, even though he did not know where he was going. When his eyes could not see what he was looking for, and his mind did not understand, he did not turn back, nor did his feet stop walking onward. God honoured his persevering faith. The greatest epitaph to Abraham is not that he started out in faith, but that he ended in faith. Hebrews 11 lists Abraham and others like him as examples of perseverance in trials. Not as people to be admired, but as examples to be followed.

The race that is before us will only be won by a finisher. Those who drop out are ineligible for the prize. Champions are not those who do not tire, nor are they those who do not feel like quitting. They are those who persevere to the end, however they feel. For perseverance is not about feelings or emotions. It is about the determination that whatever happens on the way, we will be there at the end. The end result must be of greater value than the trial itself. If it is not, we will not persevere.

James in chapter 5 uses the life of Job to illustrate perseverance. The loss of all that was close to his heart could not deter him from obeying God. When his children died, his health failed, his wealth vanished and his friends deserted him, though his understanding wavered, his perseverance did not forsake him. What he did not know and understand paled into insignificance when compared with what he did know. He knew God would never desert him. He knew the importance of enduring to the end. Unless we are confident that God is for us, we will not stick it out when circumstances appear adverse.

As a young man I was in love with the sport of triathlon. I would run and cycle almost every day, and most days swim at 6.30 a.m. before going to work. When the joy and excitement of competition became of less worth than a warm bed on a cold winter morning, I knew my days were numbered. Likewise, when the day dawns that the presence of God and likeness to Jesus becomes of less worth to us than an easy alternative to trials, it will be safe to say we've lost the fight, dropped out of the race and surrendered the crown of life.

Sadly, that is the case with some that have professed to follow Jesus, but it was certainly not the case with the Apostle Paul. He was able to write to Timothy (2 Timothy 4:7-8) that he was confident that as he neared the end of his life, he had run his race and fought his fight. Having stood his corner, he had an assurance that his crown was awaiting his entrance into heaven.

We may not know what trials await us, but we can count it as joy when they come, for we know why they come, and what will be the end result. They will take us, as we practice what God has taught us and is teaching us, on towards perfection.

CHAPTER TWO

The Danger of Doubt

But when he asks, he must believe and not doubt, because he who doubts is like a wave of the sea, blown and tossed by the wind (James 1:6).

One of the great theological debates down through the centuries of Church history has been the validity of the contribution of the Epistle of James to Christian doctrine. It is a subject constantly discussed by theologians, even as eminent as the great German reformer Martin Luther. Had he chosen the books that make up the New Testament, there is little doubt that James would not have been included.

The subject that causes the problem for so many is the subject of faith and its relationship to works. James stresses the difference between living faith and fruitless faith, a distinction that many have misinterpreted, and one that we will look at in greater detail later.

In 1:6-8 James is dealing with prayer and faith in the same context, a thread he later picks up again in chapter 5. It is evident from these references that faith is a central principle at work in the believer's life. For people like Luther, faith was the result of revelation, while to James it was the norm. Unlike Luther, who lived in an era where the validity of faith was denied, James lived among those who professed Christianity based on faith. Further to this distinction we must understand that James is not writing to those coming to faith in Christ, but to those already there. Hence the importance of dealing with doubt. If faith is the foundation on which we have built our lives, doubt is that which erodes those foundations.

That James values faith is seen in the way he deals with doubt. To him it is a key that underlies what we do and how we act. The trials we undergo are seen as a test of our faith, they are not seen as a test of our deeds. Doubt does not attack those deeds, it attacks our faith; for if it kills our faith, our deeds will wither automatically.

Another example of this is seen in the writings of Peter. When he writes of trials (1 Peter 1:6-7) it is not a man's deeds or actions that are tried but his faith. Likewise as James moves on to the practical outworking of faith we see the importance of doubt as another of the issues that face every Christian in their day to day living. Though the context is prayer, the application is universal.

The Christian cannot live out the plan and purpose of God for his life and live in doubt. He cannot fulfil his God-ordained destiny unless he first acknowledges that doubt is a genuine threat and learns how to deal with it.

Doubt finds its origin in the mind, not in the heart of a man. That this is evident is clear from the prime consequence of doubt, being double-minded. It is also noticeable that while the Bible has much to say about the mind and the heart, it draws clear distinctions. It is not to the mind that faith comes, but to the heart. As for doubt, it is vice versa.

This distinction is not meaningless, for it lays the foundation for dealing with doubt. Some would teach that doubt comes from the devil, and therefore as long as we ignore him, all will be well. We need to be more thorough with spiritual issues. We will not live out the purposes of God by wishing and hoping. The principles given in the Bible are given that we might apply them in such situations as when doubt arises.

The heart is portrayed in the Bible as being more than the vital organ of human anatomy. It is portrayed as the seat of human personality and emotion. It is the core of our being and central to our motivation. It is the part of a man that, more than all others, is the representation of the sum total of all other parts. As a man is in his heart, that is how he is. Hence the Bible talks of a clean or a pure heart, and of the desire of the heart. In Romans 10:10 Paul writes explaining that it is in the heart and not the mind that belief rests. Understanding this truth lays the foundation for dealing with doubt.

Faith may come through the organs of hearing, but it can enter the heart without first visiting the mind. Doubt is very different, for it cannot attack the heart without first coming through the mind. This is why in Romans 12:2 we see the need for the mind to be renewed. Such an experience is transforming, not because the mind then replaces the heart, but that it then protects it by filtering out, among other things, doubt. The renewed mind will not accept conclusions made solely on what others believe is a rational basis. It accepts on a basis of belief in God and His instruction.

Looking at Genesis 3 we see clear instruction on this matter. That the devil seeks to trap Adam and Eve is clearly understood, but how he goes about it is not. His plan is not a great elaborate magical and mystical performance, but a simple sowing of the seeds of doubt. He challenges them as to what God actually said, what He actually meant and as to His actual motives. The key was not the power of persuasion, but the power of doubt.

As Christians we know the power of God's Spirit dwelling within our bodies. He has access from within. He is the very treasure that we possess within these vessels of clay. The devil seeks to gain access to our hearts from outside. The doorway he seeks to use is our mind.

If the devil seeks to raise doubts and place them firmly in our mind, how does he seek to achieve his aim? We can discover this particular secret by looking at what the Bible says, and applying it to our experience.

We must set our minds on the spiritual and not the natural (Colossians 3:2). Doubts rest in our minds when we consider the natural. David looked at Goliath through spiritual eyes. He was not brave in the sense we think of today. Bravery involves risk, but for David there was no risk. He did not believe that while God was on his side, Goliath was able to harm him. Meanwhile, his brothers had watched Goliath taunt them day after day. They doubted because they looked at the natural. They did not know the power of transformation that comes from a renewed mind.

When we look in the natural sense at our circumstances we will know defeat in every area of our lives. Some areas may prosper, or appear to prosper, but as in the Parable of the Sower recorded in Matthew 13 the cares of this world will eventually choke the very life out of them. Finance is a good example. When we look with spiritual eyes our attitude towards giving will be different from when we look with natural eyes. The spiritual man sees the need of the hungry for food, the need of the homeless for shelter, the need of Christian workers for support and therefore gives over and above the amount that in the natural he could afford. The natural mind sees our own need and will constantly cry out to us to stop giving. It will not only see the unpaid bills, but it will imagine bills that do not exist and as a result curb the giving.

We saw when considering trials the importance of right motivation, and again it raises its head. Motivation heavily influences the way we see things. If our motivation is centred on God we will see things from His perspective, and not doubt. This is certain, for doubt is the result of the interpretation of circumstances through the natural senses.

The spiritual mind (and therefore the spiritual senses) is not hostile towards God. It is able to do more than just recognize the evidences of the presence of God. It understands the consequences. It understands what is not of God, and dispels the questions that lead to doubt before they can take root.

The minute the mind steps into the natural, it no longer discerns the spiritual. The mind that once prayed believing God would answer now doubts that it deserves God's help. It now doubts its place in God's family.

For a number of years I worked for a company that ran a computer programme known as 'what if'. If there were possible changes to the sales demand or material availability the programme would be run. It did more than reflect the changes; it highlighted every possible consequence. As a planning aid it was invaluable. Doubt runs a similar programme within the natural mind. It presents every 'what if' that is a consequence of God not keeping His Word, or our misunderstanding of what God has said.

As an example we look once again at finance. Doubt will prevent giving to the needy by presenting 'what ifs'. What if a bill comes? What if I lose my job? What if my car breaks down? What if my mortgage repayments increase? It casts doubt on God's ability to keep us. It doesn't ask what will happen to the hungry, or the homeless, or the unemployed. It erodes at what God expects of you, and at what you can expect of God.

Satan is still trying to cast doubt on God and what He has said. If he succeeds there, all that we hold dear becomes susceptible to doubt. Where faith looks for encouragement, doubt looks for possible other meanings and hidden agendas, casting a shadow over truth. It is the seed of most unpleasant fruit.

James speaks of being double-minded. The word he uses in the Greek language conveys the idea of having two different and separate views. This is not slight uncertainty. It is like having two individual and independent minds.

Jesus taught a similar truth. It is not possible to serve two masters. Inconsistency occurs in what we think, how we make decisions and where we place our trust. This is to be double-minded in its fullest and truest sense.

James develops the effect of being double-minded and graphically illustrates the full extent of that effect; total instability. The man who doubts becomes unstable in the same way that a wave does when it is at the mercy of the elements. He is affected by what he sees, by what he hears, and by what he feels, irrespective of the truth contained. He is deceived by what he perceives, and every effort he makes to avoid a current in the great ocean of Christian experience, leaves him more exposed and more vulnerable.

God cannot build upon instability, just as the unstable cannot receive what is necessary for growth. Whatever God lays before them will be subject to the doubt that rules their mind. Yet stability is a vital part of God's plan for His people.

The New Testament uses the illustration of a building to express how God is working within His Church. As Christians we form a building that is not made by human hands, but constructed by God. Such a building is dependent upon the stability of each relevant component in order to stand.

There is a sense of inevitability that barrenness will follow closely after instability. If, as Hebrews 11:6 tells us, it is not possible to please God without faith, it must be impossible to please Him with doubt. This is an important principle that should never be far from the front of our minds. Without pleasing God we are not going to experience fulfilment and abundance of blessing. This is not because God is a vindictive God, but because of the way man is created.

The normal Christian life is a life of blessing. A life therefore that does not bear the hallmark of blessing is a life that needs to be re-examined. One issue that must be considered is doubt. One of the key reasons that at times many of us struggle with unanswered prayer, or encounter difficulties in coping with the situations that confront us, is that doubt exists in our minds.

This can be difficult for the Christian, for it confuses what is of God and what is not. Unanswered prayer because of doubt is different to the times when God desires that we tarry or persist in prayer. Such times exist, where God is testing our motives and our determination. When this is the case, we are not disheartened by waiting, but hope and expectancy strengthens our spirit. Our prayers are constant and unwavering because our spirit relates to God's Spirit and understands what is taking place.

Doubt does not cause us to persevere, it causes us to quit. It does not fill our life with hope and expectancy but drains it of all we have. For if doubt leads to instability and instability leads to barrenness, barrenness leads to disillusionment. Many that backslide can trace the turning point to doubt. It may pass through a host of stages, raise its head in a vast array of ways, but in many cases, behind the scenes, casting its devilish influence is doubt.

Disillusionment does not come as the result of understanding truth, it comes as a result of a wrong perception of truth. A perception that doubts that truth is what it actually is. If experiences we go through leave us bitter and angry, it is possible we are suffering because somewhere along the line we have started to doubt. Even in cases where we were wronged, the hurt can be the result of doubt. Someone may launch an attack on us, but how we react is not about them, it is about us. If we doubt that God is interested in us, that He is overseeing our lives and loves us, what others say about us and do to us can take on added importance. We can refer back to the story of Joseph. What others did to him didn't pull him down to their level, but lifted him up to God's.

As obvious as it sounds, the way to deal with doubt is to believe. This is not just true of prayer, but of every area and corner of our lives. Faith can dispel doubt just as doubt can dispel truth. The deciding factor is often where our minds are set. This is not a case of 'mind over matter', or positive thinking, this is a renewed mind at work. If our minds are set on spiritual things, faith will triumph.

As Christians we are spiritual people, and must live on a spiritual level. It is the way God has chosen for us to live. As for whether we live in such a manner, our minds hold one of the keys. If we allow doubt to rule our thinking, we will fall short of what God has deemed to be the normal way of life for the believer.

We should notice too, that the Bible doesn't teach us to leave this to God, but rather tells us to take the responsibility ourselves. We are told to 'set' our own minds on spiritual matters in Colossians 3:2, and in 1 Peter 1:13 to 'prepare' our minds. We can take control of situations that we may fear, by doing what God commands, and taking control of our own minds. James is challenging his readers to believe and not doubt. This is not something others will do for them, they must do it for themselves.

We renew our minds by looking at the past. We remember God's goodness, mercy, compassion and grace. We remember the victories He has won for us, the times He picked us up when we fell, the times He fed us when we were hungry. We remind ourselves of His saving, healing and life-giving power. God is no less a God today than He was in the past.

In the same way we can renew ourselves by reminding ourselves of the future. We remind ourselves that our destiny is tied up in His plan and purpose. If we doubt that truth, all that we have done to this point will devalue in worth. Much of our spent time will have become wasteful pursuit. We know in whom it is that we have put our trust and are persuaded of His ability to keep His promises.

This is more than positive thinking, and certainly not wishful thinking. This is faith thinking. Look at raffle or lottery tickets as examples. Some may buy tickets as a means to helping charities, others because they consider it possible they will win substantial prizes. People may believe they will win a million pounds, but enough doubt exists within their minds that they don't give their jobs up before they win.

Faith is not believing we could, it is believing God will. It is not built upon probability or possibility, but upon something real and tangible. Hebrews chapter 11 gives us great insight into faith. It shows from the outset of the chapter that faith is real, it not only has substance, but is itself the substance on which a God-pleasing life is built. We see too, that the city for which Abraham looked had foundations. It was real. Though it was not evident to others, it was not a figment of Abraham's imagination. It was very real.

Some paint the picture of faith and doubt as being the opposite sides of the scales, which tip in favour of one side or the other based upon the evidence available. This gives a false portrayal of the relationship between faith and doubt. Faith is not one side of the scales, it is the scales. Truth and doubt may be the sides, but it is faith that decides. It is faith that chooses. Faith determines whether we accept doubt or whether we act upon truth.

We must look at God's Word as more than a collection of stories or moral codes. We must learn to discern truth from its pages. We must not just look for facts and statistics, but we must search out truth. Jesus was critical of the religious rulers in the Gospels, not least because of their lack of understanding of the Scriptures. They dedicated their lives to learning words and facts but could not discern truth.

Such truth applied to our minds will dispel doubt. Truth sets us free. It sets us free from all things at all times. Included in that all encompassing statement is doubt. In liberating our minds, truth becomes the substance on which our faith is founded.

Prayer may be the easiest thing in the world, but the manner in which we approach God should not be taken for granted. We will not ask of God without doubt, unless we first prepare our hearts and minds. Such preparation will have a dramatic effect.

If one of the keys to the Christian life is to be constantly living in communion and communication with God, we must be constantly in a state of preparation. We cannot attempt to create certain times when doubt is banished, it must be a way of life. To know the constant blessing and generosity of God in our lives, we must be always ready to approach in faith, the God who gives without measure.

The context of which James writes in 1:5 is that of wisdom, but the principle is greater than any one aspect of our lives. God desires that we all have wisdom, not because He desires wise children, but complete children. Doubt is a major obstacle to our pursuit of perfection. Whatever we lack we can receive; whatever hinders can be overcome; whoever opposes can be defeated. Yet none of this can take place while doubt holds sway over our minds and our hearts. We cannot be complete, we cannot be fulfilled and we cannot realize our destiny while doubt exists in our lives, and gives birth to the barrenness of unanswered prayer.

Let us therefore with renewed minds, banish doubt and ask in faith, believing that we will receive the blessing of answered prayer.

CHAPTER THREE

Understanding Temptation

When tempted, no-one should say, 'God is tempting me.' For God cannot be tempted by evil, nor does he tempt anyone; but each one is tempted when, by his own evil desire, he is dragged away and enticed. Then, after desire has conceived, it gives birth to sin; and sin, when it is full-grown, gives birth to death (James 1:13-15).

James continues along the theme of dealing with the big issues confronting believers by tackling the subject of temptation. This is a subject that many have difficulty understanding, not least because of the confusion that often arises in defining the difference between temptation and trials. Certainly the word used in the original by James can be translated as either, and by some translators it is used as either and both. It could be that the lesson we need to learn is not just understanding the literal meaning of what James writes, but the circumstances in which it applies to us.

It is important to understand that the difference between a trial and a temptation is largely seen in the context in which they arise within our lives; rather than in a grammatical or theological difference. Some would teach that trials offer the possibility of temptation in the sense that they offer the possibility of failing God and His declared standards. The context of which James writes is distinctly different but not necessarily contrary to this teaching.

What does it mean to be tempted? In the English language, it is usually defined as being offered an object or a course of action that is attractive. Sometimes it is used in the context of something forbidden or ill-advised. A person may be 'tempted' to finish work early and watch a football match, while a person on a strict diet may be 'tempted' to eat a cream cake. Yet another may see an open till in an empty shop and be 'tempted' to help themselves. These illustrations show the wide scope of the use of the word. The first example does not involve wrongdoing, nor does it involve what is necessarily an unwise course of action, merely the existence of a choice and a preference. The second example shows nothing more than what might be unwise rather than wrong; while the third shows what is clearly wrongdoing.

In the biblical context, the definition of temptation is much narrower. It is seen as the offering of something that is an alternative to the will of God. It is probable that such an alternative would prove attractive to the senses and possibly logical to the mind, but the key is not the presentation of the alternative, but its very existence. Any alternative to the plan and desires of God must by definition set themselves against God.

It is vitally important that every believer understands temptation, for sin is the greatest problem we face. It is the reason for Christmas; it is the reason for Easter. It is the very reason that God sent His Son into the world to die, and even though we know that as a result of His death our sins have been dealt with, we live in a sinful world. A world that we are not called to avoid, but to live in, and to do so in the same manner as did Jesus during His earthly ministry. As we seek to follow the example of Jesus we must also consider that He lived a sinless life, conquering temptation on every occasion it arose.

The Christian will not be perfect this side of heaven, but he should be a person who knows how to deal with temptation. The New Testament writers acknowledge openly the weakness of human nature and the ease with which temptation can overtake us, but they emphasize too, the need for holy living; a way of life not possible for those who cannot conquer temptation.

The importance Jesus placed upon this subject is evident in His teaching. If our eyes cause us to offend, to be tempted and yield to temptation, it would be better to be blind. However much we try to 'spiritualize' the meaning of such teaching, it was meant to be understood at its face value. It means exactly what it says. Secondary interpretations are exactly what they sound, secondary. This shows exactly the level of importance Jesus placed upon the need of His followers to understand temptation and therefore avoid sin.

We must understand the source of temptation. James makes this clear with a very powerful statement. Not only can God not be tempted, but also it is not in His nature to be a source of temptation. God cannot sin. If He cannot be tempted, He cannot sin. To understand this fully we need to understand both God and sin and their respective natures. Sin is selfish. It bases itself upon a desire to promote personal benefit above the purposes of God. For James this is abundantly clear. Yielding to temptation is the following after personal desire. In the sense in which James is writing, God does not have personal desires. Love is intrinsically selfless; it never promotes itself, but rather promotes the well-being of its recipients. If God is love (1 John 4:16), then He cannot possess selfish desires. He must be selfless. That this is true is clearly evident from His mercy and gifts to mankind.

James takes this point and unfolds it. We receive all the good that we do, because of the selfless life and giving of God. He cannot be tempted because His nature cannot experience temptation. His very being is selfless and perfect. In being selfless, there is no possibility of temptation.

This leads us to the question of Jesus Christ and the

temptations He experienced at the hand of the devil. In Luke 4:1-13 we are given the raw facts of this experience. The Son of God, both divine and human in nature is tempted. The very nature of this experience reflects the reality and vulnerability of the humanity of Jesus, rather than possible imperfections in His divinity. Luke's record shows with great clarity the source of the temptations. For though it was with the Spirit's accompaniment He entered the wilderness, it was not from God that the temptations came. The God that cannot be tempted, cannot be the source of our temptation.

These two truths go hand in hand. If they did not, then the character and nature of God would contain great inconsistencies. A holy God could not desire anything short of holiness in His followers. We should consider this point further, for how we understand it will determine how we act and react with regard to temptation.

In Matthew 6:9-13 we read the Lord's Prayer, the prayer Jesus taught His disciples to pray. He teaches His followers to ask God not to lead them into temptation. What does He mean? Is He asking them to ask God not to do something He cannot do anyway? It is already clear that God cannot tempt us, so there must be significance in the request we see Jesus making. He is identifying an important distinction, a distinction between temptation and what precedes it. Trials are not temptations, but they can be the forerunners. The Lord's Prayer encourages us to pray that God will lead our footsteps away from the path that leads to temptation. Trials are a part of God's plan for our lives, but temptation, as James sees it, certainly is not.

If God cannot be the source of temptation, then the Christian should not be the source of temptation to others. Our actions and our words should make it easy for people to live holy lives. We should provoke people into holy living, rather than into anger, jealousy, temptation and sin.

Having pointed out that God cannot be tempted and that He cannot tempt another, James locks the door on this point by showing that God's nature is unchanging. He uses the illustration of a sundial. The movement of shadows reflects change, and the dial reflects the change by measuring it as time. God is eternal; He is outside of time. Time measures change, God does not change, therefore time does not apply to Him. It is a simple equation, but reflects the nature of God. He is today what He was yesterday and will be for every tomorrow. The God that cannot tempt you today will not tempt you tomorrow.

James goes on to explain that while temptation does not come from God, man himself is not altogether blameless. The first reaction of human nature is to pass the blame on to someone else. Here James pre-empts such a reaction. The blame lies firmly with man. How easy it is to give in to natural desires and blame others. Easy, but not right.

Having established man's vulnerability, we should note too the devil's involvement. We make much of the doctrine of sin in regard to human nature, and the abuse of the freedom of choice that God gave to mankind. Yet we often fight shy of the role of the devil in sin. Either we apportion to him total blame or no blame at all.

We can look at the Garden of Eden for help and enlightenment. It was through the devil that temptation takes reality, but it was in the mind and then the heart of Adam and Eve that the reality of temptation became the reality of sin.

As far as temptation is concerned we must be aware that the suggestions and opportunities that present themselves before us originated in the pit of darkest hell. Unless we grasp such a truth, temptation will seem attractive and in our minds become a viable alternative to what God desires for us. Unless we grasp this truth, temptation and the sin that may follow will never become abhorrent to us.

Once we understand the source of temptation we need to comprehend the cause of temptation. The key to this is knowing where we belong. The man who is tempted is a man who is taken away from his natural, or rather his 'spiritual' environment.

James shows this by the use of two words that could well be borrowed from fishing and hunting. The first word is 'dragged', which could easily be used of a fish that is pulled out of the water by an angler. The second word 'enticed' could just as easily be used of an animal that has been tricked out of its den or lair. Both words convey much the same idea.

As a teenager I had a brief flirtation with the sport of fishing. During one of many unsuccessful expeditions to a local river, I managed to hook a trout. Dreams of a fish tea were dashed, for although it had found its way to my hook, I lacked the necessary skill, cunning and composure to bring it back to the side of the river still attached to the hook. It fought its way to freedom. Once out of the water it would have been mine.

Believers who are trapped by temptation will all have at least one thing in common. They will have been enticed away from the place they once belonged. Some will even have left without a struggle.

From where does temptation drag us? The answer may be twofold. Firstly we are removed from the plan of God for our lives. Our attention will have been taken away from the lives we are called to live. Secondly we are then removed from the presence of God.

To understand this fully we should read carefully what James has written. There is an act of enticement. Distraction from the things of God is the start. Not fixing our minds single-mindedly upon the call of God that we have each received, will see us led into temptation. This may in some cases be made worse by a poor understanding of that calling. Such people may need little distracting, for they may not even be sure of where they should be living and looking.

Once our minds and eyes are suffering such distraction, the yielding to temptation will be made easier by leaving the presence of God.

If God is ever present, how can we leave His presence? The question is a valid one and also one that is difficult for some to understand. God does not abandon us because we fail Him. A yielding to temptation will not see His Spirit leave our lives. Yet we should consider that it is possible to be in God's presence and neither appreciate it, nor enjoy it. Distraction can rob us of all that God's presence should mean to us. Sin can become obsessive. Pursuing evil becomes more important than the One in whose presence we live and to whom we owe our very existence.

At such times we no longer 'experience' God's presence for we are no longer aware of it. In short, temptation drags our mind further away from God, and our awareness of Him and His presence.

Living in ignorance of our weak and vulnerable points is a dangerous practice. Some of us are vulnerable because we think we are not. It is not that we should be preoccupied with human weakness, it is rather that we should take steps to strengthen ourselves. We do this by avoiding situations that could exploit our weaknesses, and by applying scriptural principles to such weaknesses, that they might become our strengths.

The Christian life is not a game. Avoiding sin is neither a hobby nor an option. It is deadly serious, with the emphasis being on deadly. Distraction can lead to conception, which in turn leads to sin and therefore death. The man of God is not only a man that recognizes the importance of holiness, but also the power and effect of temptation. He is a man who takes avoidance of temptation and sin very seriously.

Once we recognize the need to avoid temptation, we must consider how we avoid it. If temptation relies upon our attention being turned away from God, we must ensure that we guard against complacency. Paul warns us of such a danger in 1 Corinthians 10:12 where he writes, 'So, if you think you are standing firm, be careful that you don't fall!' Distraction from spiritual matters comes to us all, but most frequently to those prepared for and awaiting distraction.

In the life of David the great king of Israel we have a vivid example. Though greatly blessed by God, this man of faith and insight falls into an adulterous encounter with a beautiful woman, and enters into a murderous plan. The story is told quite graphically in 2 Samuel 11. David sees a very beautiful woman and is distracted by her looks. The distraction leads to conception, and sin and death follow. There are many valid points that come from this story, but one salient point is found at the beginning of the chapter. It was the time when kings went out to war, but David stayed at home! Had he been where he should have been, history would have recorded a different story.

It is said that John Wesley's mother would remind her sons of the devil's ability to find work for idle hands. This is advice that would stand us all in good stead. Many have fallen into temptation and sin because they have been distracted and drawn away from where they should have been. There is not one of us that can take his shoulder from the plough without risking a greater chance of temptation. Unless our lives are consumed by a passion for God we will know and struggle with temptation. That is not to say that servants of God are immune from temptation, but they will recognize their own vulnerability and prepare themselves accordingly.

We have already seen from Luke 4 that Jesus was prepared for temptation. He was accompanied by the Holy Spirit and armed with the Scriptures. We cannot underestimate the importance of either. Being accompanied by the Holy Spirit in every avenue of our lives is vital for power over temptation, but we also need the power of God's Word.

Jesus knew more than the words of the Scriptures, He knew their meaning, and how to apply them to His life. He recognized the power they possess. He didn't flee, panic or worry. He simply applied the Scriptures.

The devil makes it his business to ensure that temptation will find its way to our door. It is our responsibility to ensure that the door is firmly closed, and stays closed. There may be aspects of temptation that we cannot control or influence, e.g. it was not David's fault a beautiful woman was bathing within his range of sight, but there are two key factors that we can control.

The first is our own vulnerability. We have already noted that David had no control over Bathsheba's bathing habits, but he did have control over where he was, and where his eyes were pointed. We are responsible for our lives and our lifestyles. Where and among whom we spend our lives is our choice. To spend time where temptation is greatest is unwise, and is contrary to the teaching of the Scriptures. Action to avoid temptation is better in the eyes of God than the prayer requesting forgiveness for yielding to it.

The second factor that emerges is the closeness of our relationship with God. The life lived in the spiritual realm is aware of the enemy's plans as well as vulnerable situations. A close relationship with God also safeguards our motives and intentions. The closer we are to God in our daily walk, the more transparent are our lives.

We are already starting to see the importance of right motivation. This is a vital key in victory over temptation. The one sure way to triumph over temptation is to be motivated by a love for God. As we submit to God, and accept His Lordship over our lives we are showing resistance to the devil. The result of such actions, James tells us, is that he will flee from us.

It is vital that we develop a lifestyle that is resistant to the devil. We are not ignorant of his methods, and must develop resistance accordingly. It is not that we live in fear of him, or are preoccupied by him. It is that as we submit to God, considering Him in all we do, we will experience victory.

Jesus taught in Luke 22:46 that prayer is an important weapon in fighting temptation. Why? Because it is part of the process of submission to God and His will. We should consider too that it produces the right spiritual conditions for us to know the Holy Spirit's power and presence. Such conditions make it easy for God to speak to us through His Word.

We must learn to challenge our motives and be honest with ourselves. If we cannot be honest with ourselves, how can we be honest with God?

There is one fundamental fact that we should bring to the surface of our lives. Temptation is more than a personal battle within the believer. It is a spiritual battle between God, the devil and the whole of the Church on earth. Make no mistake, while the devil is battling against you, God is fighting for you, and the whole of the Church of Christ on earth is affected by your actions. Every time a believer, wherever in the world they are, resists temptation, the Church knows victory!

Victory over temptation is God's will for our lives. It should be the norm for the believer. However deeply we may feel we are trapped, repentance and a yielding to God's Spirit have to be the starting point for deliverance, but they are not the end. We must endeavour to know continual submission to the will of God, and live to the standards He expects of us. This is not a legalistic obedience to set laws, but the responsibility of Grace. To continue in sin is to deny the power of God over it.

Some Christians are deceived into believing that if they resist the devil they will stir him up and make matters worse. To believe such a lie is to settle for a poor imitation of Christianity. Christ has won a total victory over the devil. It is not possible for him to influence us against our will. This is precisely the point that James is making.

We are called to be victorious. What are we meant to be victorious over? The answer is obvious, the devil and temptation. We must not offend a righteous and holy God. We must not weaken our testimony. We must live lives that are prepared for battle and ready for victory.

CHAPTER FOUR

Hearers and Doers

Do not merely listen to the word, and so deceive yourselves. Do what it says. Anyone who listens to the word but does not do what it says is like a man who looks at his face in a mirror and, after looking at himself, goes away and immediately forgets what he looks like. But the man who looks intently into the perfect law that gives freedom, and continues to do this, not forgetting what he has heard, but doing it – he will be blessed in what he does (James 1:22-25).

James, in the previous verse to the passage quoted above, sets the level of importance that is to be placed upon God's Word. He tells his readers that God's Word is able to save them, and the word he uses to describe the saving power of God is the very word used in Matthew 1:21 to describe the mission of Jesus. It is not only because it saves that God's Word should be reverenced. It should be treated with the greatest respect because of whose it is – God's.

I believe that the words James recorded almost 2,000 years ago under the inspiration and influence of the Holy Spirit are as relevant today as in any other era of history. Possibly they are more relevant today in the light of the theoretical Christianity that many adhere to, especially in the very logical and rational thinking Western World.

We saw at the outset of this book that Christianity is something that is real and tangible. Jesus preached a message that worked, that was real, that had effects. If His message is still true it will still change lives even today.

The Bible is mistreated if it is treated as nothing more than a reference book for Christian morality or philosophy. It is living and vibrant, and as James points out, can bring about salvation. It can meet the greatest need a man can know. It brings a man into relationship with God. It sets him free of his sin, his guilt, and his fears. It can only do this because of its author, and its living and vibrant nature.

God does not declare His Word to furnish men with facts and figures. He does so to touch lives, to heal, to comfort, to console and to befriend. God declares His Word because He is a God who cares, but also because He is a God who communicates.

James presents us all with a timely reminder of the importance of hearing what God has to say. This is not a multiple-choice question. It is not a case of hearing or doing. We cannot become doers until we become hearers.

In James 1:19 we are encouraged to control our faculties. We must give priority to listening over speaking. James is acutely aware of the need to listen. It is no accident that God gave us two ears and only one mouth. The reason is of far greater importance than facial symmetry.

Jesus on a number of occasions made a particular challenge to His hearers. He challenged those who had ears to actually hear what He was saying. A strange challenge? Not if you hear what He was saying. There is a significant difference between hearing the words and hearing their meaning.

James describes the man who hears the Word as someone who looks into a mirror, sees his own reflection and recognizes it. At this point he knows who he is. He hears the Word and recognizes its source, origin and importance.

The Christian walk is dependent upon hearing God. In John 10 we have one of the great discourses of Jesus. He talks of His followers as being sheep and Himself as being the 'Good Shepherd'. His sheep recognize His voice. Sheep do not recognize the shepherd by his looks, his aftershave, his clothes or even his mannerisms. They recognize the voice. It is not possible to remain a follower of Jesus and not recognize His voice.

Some will trust Jesus for salvation, but they will not follow Him. It is one thing to stay within the sheep-pen and trust the shepherd for security, but it is not enough. Safety is important, but the pasture so necessary to sustain growth and life is outside the pen. This being the case the sheep's life may well depend on two things, the skill of the shepherd and whether it recognizes the shepherd's voice.

The life that God has called us to live is a life that is dependent upon Him leading us. How can we be led unless we can firstly hear His voice, and secondly recognize whose voice it is? We are living in days when there are many voices. We must be able to discern their origins. Knowing the voice of God is not a special gift reserved for certain people; it is an essential part of the believer's life.

In 2 Peter 1:18 and 1 John 1:1 two of the early Christian leaders wrote to fellow believers explaining that their faith was built upon what they had heard personally. They had heard and recognized the voice of God. They were present when God spoke from heaven and in acknowledging His Son, gave the command to listen to what He had to say (Mark 9:7).

Paul, another of the great early Christian leaders, like Peter and John, knew the importance of being a hearer of the Word. He explains in Romans 10:17 that faith comes through hearing, not through achieving, nor through thinking; not even through speaking, but simply through hearing.

This leaves us with an important question. When we sit under the sound of preaching and teaching, do we actually hear what God is saying? When we read His Word do we actually hear His voice? If not, why not?

We have a God that speaks, that communicates. Just for a

moment consider the time and effort that went into the Old
Testament sacrificial system. All of this time and effort shows
exactly how important it was to God that the nation heard and
understood what He was saying. Special offerings, sacrifices,
ceremonial clothing, special days all had to be set apart and
observed to the finest detail. Yet we can simply close our lips
and open our ears.

We should consider even further the work of the Holy Spirit.
Even the Gifts of the Holy Spirit that we see recorded in 1
Corinthians 12, depend for their effectiveness on our willingness
to hear what the Holy Spirit is saying. What value is there in
God sending a prophetic message, or supernatural Words of
Wisdom or Knowledge advising and encouraging us, if we are
not listening? We only have to look back at the sufferings of the
nation of Israel in the Old Testament to see the results of not
listening. Some of their misery came about because they were
not doers of the Word, but other sufferings, because they were
not hearers either.

It is not possible to maintain any relationship without
communication. People who are deaf have to lip-read, learn sign
language or read written notes in order to communicate. Why
do they go to such lengths? The answer is as obvious as the
question is silly. To maintain a relationship there has to be two-
way communications. Where the ears are not able to hear, the
eyes have to work twice as hard.

It is obvious therefore, that we cannot maintain a relationship
with a living God, unless we can hear His voice. Reading the
text of the Bible is not enough. It is not that the Bible does not
contain everything we need to find and sustain life, it is rather
that we need to 'hear' the meaning not the sound of the words.
The same God who breathed life into mankind way back in the
account of Creation, needs to breathe the same life into the
words as we read them.

Having seen the importance of hearing God's Word we must become doers also. To hear and not act upon what we have heard is to fall well short of God's plan and purpose for our lives. The purpose of the epistle James has written is to show that Christianity is more than a theory, it is real and practical. God's Word is not about a set of theories; it is about a set of instructions.

To James, not to act on what has been heard is sheer folly. It is as absurd as a man looking at his own reflection in a mirror, and going away and picking up a picture of himself and not knowing who it is. That is precisely what James is saying.

Christianity is not about attending a church. It is not about listening to sermons. They are a part, and only a part. It is about putting into practice what we see and hear. It is not a weekly visit to church; it is a daily walk with God. It is a day on day personal journey of experiencing the reality of what God is saying coming true and working in our lives.

The whole purpose of looking into God's Word and hearing His voice is for it to affect us; to make a difference in our lives. To merely listen is to deceive ourselves. If we think that we can experience God moving in our lives in power and authority and not contribute by way of obedience, then we are self-deluded.

God requires us to be obedient. In God's eyes it is better to be obedient than to make great sacrifices. Obedience to what God says is vital for growth and development. The sheep that hears the shepherd's voice but does not do what he says is very quickly going to form a part of a wolf's diet. It is the shepherd's responsibility to lead, but it is the sheep's responsibility to follow. Many are quick to criticize the leader, but the truth is that sometimes the real problem lies with the follower.

We have a responsibility as the children of God to put into practice what He teaches us. In Luke 8:21 Jesus makes it abundantly clear who His family are. They are those who hear what God is saying, and do it.

The man who does what he hears God saying is a wise man. In Luke 6:47-49 Jesus gives a now famous illustration. The man who hears what God is saying and obeys the words is likened to a wise man, who when he built a house, did so on a sure foundation. Whatever rain and wind may beat down, his home is safe. The foolish man did the opposite. He does not do what God has said. When the elements beat down, his house falls down because the foundation is weak.

As the Church we have to consider why people who once ran well are hindered in going onwards. One reason must surely be that they suddenly start to build the foundation of their Christian life on sand. They no longer are doers of the Word.

We must not underestimate the importance of obedience in the eyes of God. The verse preceding the illustration of the wise and foolish builders is a very important one. In it Jesus asks those listening why they address Him as 'Lord' but do not do what He commands. Verbal assent which is not backed up with obedience is of little value.

However dedicated to God we may feel we are, we cannot be obedient in theory. Our calling is not to know, but to live. Jesus did not come to this world as a babe that we might have knowledge, He came that we might have life. His desire is that we might learn from His life, example and teaching. Yet He did not teach for teaching's sake. It was so that the life He gives might be received and sustained. ·

Irrespective of what we might say or sing in church each week, it is what happens outside that is the test of our Christianity. It is right that we should meet together. It is right that we should pray and worship together. It is also right that we should proclaim the Lordship of Jesus by our actions as well as our words.

Perhaps some of us need to be reminded that 'doing' does not always involve great physical feats. Rarely does God ask us to perform such duties as routing the armies of foreign invaders. It is not every day we are called to perform acts of faith on a national scale. While every problem that you and I face might not be a Philistine warrior called Goliath, it might be a giant by another name. Day by day we are called to be obedient to God whatever the circumstances and whatever the opposition. Your giant might be a person; it might be a phobia, a habit, a bill or even an illness. It is not the size of the task that counts, but the fact that we use faith to accomplish it. We can stand in every circumstance, but we will not stand at all unless we are doers of the Word.

There are many times within our Christian experience when blessing is thwarted, growth stunted and life complicated, simply because we do not do what God has asked us to do. The whole purpose of His communicating with mankind is that we might know what to do and what to be.

In the previous chapters we have spoken about trials, doubt and temptation. Already we have seen in these subjects the importance of putting what we know into practice. In view of the difficulties and challenges that we all face daily, theory is not enough. We need to live out a practical Christianity.

We must also be aware that the instruction we receive from God is perfect. Perfect not only because it originates in God, but also perfect because it is complete in itself. It needs no addition or subtraction. We need no other argument, discussion or explanation. God's Word is enough. Whether His spoken Word or His written Word, it is perfect. The only way we can follow after perfection in our walk with God is to follow His perfect instruction, by doing as well as hearing.

As we have looked at the importance of being a doer of the Word we have noted that doing and obeying seem to be interchangeable. The difference between 'hearing' and 'hearing and doing', is not necessarily the action, but the intention.

God's Word is able to discern the intentions of our heart. He honours the intent above the action. This should be reassuring to all believers who at sometime or other have experienced the best of intentions going horribly wrong. This is not an excuse to do nothing, but a realization that God does not honour the right thing done for the wrong reason as often man does. Someone who does good to be seen of men will have a reward, but it will not be in heaven.

There is a great reward of blessing to the man who with honest intentions puts what he has heard into practice. This is a principle that we should all weave into the fabric of our lives. Obedience to God always brings blessing. Jesus taught it to His disciples, 'Now that you know these things, you will be blessed if you do them' (John 13:17).

It is strange to think that though Christians understand they should be blessed, not all know what it means. The word recorded in John 13:17 in the Greek text carries with it the idea of enlargement. To grow and to gain, that is the nature of blessing. It is more than being happy. There are those who do not understand that blessing is fulfilment, it is more than happiness.

God's blessing enlarges us spiritually, causing our lives to grow and to gain accordingly. This is illustrated clearly in the life of Abraham. God took him and blessed him mightily and marvellously. He enlarged him and stretched him and filled his life with good things. Though aged and unable to bear a son, God made Sarah's womb fruitful. He gave to Abraham and Sarah, not a family, but a nation. He made his offspring a blessing to others. Abraham knew prosperity and fruitfulness, but not without being a doer and not just a hearer of the Word of God.

We talk much and often about spiritual growth. For some it has become a subject more discussed than sought after. The man that grows is a blessed man. We cannot make ourselves spiritually bigger, but blessing stretches and enlarges us. Once blessed and enlarged we do not return to our previous size. It is God who enlarges us, but it is our responsibility to live in a manner that God delights to bless and therefore causes us to grow.

Another reward of the man who is a doer of the Word is that he lives forever. In 1 John 2:17 we read that everything that is material and a part of the fabric of this world will pass away. Possessions, hopes and ambitions alike will disappear. The man who carries out God's purposes, he will live eternally. This truth is a cornerstone of the Christian Faith.

The relevance of the life we live should be seen in the context of the life that is to come. We cannot see this life as an end in itself. If we do we will fall short of God's expectancy for our lives. What we do and say must have eternal values. It is not in this world we are called to lay up our treasure. It is not in this world that we will give account to the Creator of our souls. It is not by this world's standards that we will be judged.

Our calling is an eternal calling. A calling to deal with eternal issues and situations. We should not be distracted by the material things of this world, which the Bible tells us are fading away, but concentrate on building on an eternal foundation. We cannot take material possessions from this world to the next, but we can lay up for ourselves treasure in heaven. The only eternally guaranteed investment is obedience.

Listening to God's Word will have eternal benefits once we act upon what we have heard. From time to time, each of us should consider the contribution within our lives to our eternal reward. However much treasure we have laid up in heaven, one certainty exists, it got there as a result of doing, not by hearing alone.

CHAPTER FIVE

Worthy Worship

Religion that God our Father accepts as pure and faultless is . . . (James 1:27).

Everyone that I meet seems to have an opinion on religion. Whether it is a view on what they think religion is, or what they think it ought to be, a view is usually held and often expressed. So it has been throughout the greater part of the last two thousand years. Some have held views so strong that they have been martyred for their faith. In fact, throughout the history of Christianity, a countless multitude, numbered only in heaven, have died for their beliefs. Some died during barbaric persecution, others as a result of what were deemed to be 'religious wars'. Others still were brutally and sadistically murdered because their beliefs were unacceptable and challenged those around them. Such atrocities are still a part of life for Christians in some parts of the world today.

While strong views on the subject are held by some, others have views so weak that they appear indifferent. There is no evidence of any conviction shown in the way they conduct their lives. Each person therefore draws his or her own, if somewhat differing conclusions.

Even within mainstream Christianity there will be differences. Differences in understanding and differences in practice. In a free western democratic society we are encouraged to think for ourselves and draw our own conclusions. This is well and good and obviously the envy of those not fortunate to live in such freedom. What if, however, those conclusions are wrong?

There is one factor that is often ignored when conclusions are made regarding religion. The factor is a simple one, an obvious, though overlooked one. It is the God factor. What does God think about religion?

It must be that His view is the most important one; in fact it is the only one that matters. Whatever the point under discussion, God's Word is not only of primary importance, it is the final word. Within the Bible we see examples of people who lived with no consideration of God. They are not remembered for their individuality, or their independence. They are remembered as being fools. The wise man consults God before he draws his conclusions.

Here we see James bringing such a point to the attention of his readers. We cannot follow a leader unless we know what that leader expects of us. Following God is no different. We must take His thoughts into our own consideration.

James is not writing about doctrine and creeds. Religion is not about theory, but the practical outworking of the things we believe. The word used in the Greek text for religion conveys the idea of outward acts of worship. It could easily be used of ceremonies or rituals. The context then, is clearly not theory or theology but the outward display of what we believe. A living demonstration of a living faith and worship.

As we consider religion as James sees it we must consider worship in its widest sense. We must see it as the living out of what we believe, rather than just the singing of psalms, hymns and spiritual songs to God that often forms the basis of the weekly worship in our church services. This is twenty-four hours a day, seven days a week, fifty-two weeks a year Christianity. Worship here is seen as everything we do and say.

One fascination that I have had since my childhood is looking around museums and art galleries. I love to visit such places, probably more out of curiosity than understanding. If there is one particular feature that always intrigues me, it is the statues and sculptures that are on display. While I have absolutely no appreciation of the finer points of art in general or sculptures in particular, there is one thing that always catches my eye. They may be inanimate and motionless, but some convey vibrancy and life while others look what they are, lumps of clay that are shaped into an image from the sculptor's mind. The difference is not in the material but the hand and eye of its creator.

Here James is making a similar comparison regarding the lives of those who profess to be Christians. The true believer's life and worship is living and vibrant, not motionless and static. It responds to the creativity of the One who breathes life into its being. This is why God is not seeking praise that is tied to the formality of ritual and habit, but from hearts that have been moved by His presence, and which touch the hearts of others accordingly. If we are alive, how can our worship be dead? If our Christianity is exciting, how can our worship be boring? If our Christianity is spontaneous, how can our worship be predictable?

Worship should be built upon what God is and what He desires. Therefore its foundation has to be the receiving of God's Word and acting upon it accordingly. Even in worship we must follow God's pattern. Our worship will depend upon our view of God and the condition of our lives before Him.

This is why for James speech is an important indicator to the validity of our worship. As with the life of a believer, his speech should be consistent with what is expected of a follower of Jesus. The man that compromises his speech compromises his worship. The man that lacks the self-control to control his speech cannot control his tongue in worship. Later in the epistle James picks up the subject of speech again, but to ignore the importance of the subject in the context of worship is to do so at our own peril.

We cannot worship with our lips too much or too often, but there must be a consistency between what we do and what we say. Unless there is such a consistency, our worship is neither true nor pure. If we consider what James has written, not all worship is in fact true or pure. We must ensure that such a warning does not apply to us.

This is sensitive ground, because of the intensely personal nature of worship and prayer alike. There is a strong relationship between the two, and many principles will apply equally to both. They will both start in the quiet place; a place where an individual meets with his God. No one else watching or listening, just alone with God. Though worship may begin there, it certainly doesn't end there. What develops in the secrecy and privacy of such a place should have visible and tangible effects. If we look at a man who truly knows how to worship God, we will be looking at a man whose actions and life are a total act of worship.

If the words that leave our lips and the meditations that rise from our hearts as an offering of worship are indeed a sacrifice of praise, how much more should our actions carry the same message of thankfulness? We have a great responsibility to worship God. As we read the Psalms we cannot help but to be challenged as to our worship. Time after time we are exhorted and encouraged to worship and to praise.

While we have a responsibility to worship God, because He deserves our worship, we have a further responsibility to worship God in a fitting and apt manner. God is worthy of our praise, but is our praise worthy of God?

The Old Testament records the manner in which God instructed the sacrifices were to be made. It was the responsibility of those offering the sacrifice to ensure that the sacrifice was fitting and appropriate. It is not enough to take the attitude that you will do it your way. When Jesus prayed prior to dying at Calvary, His prayer was not that He might do it His way, but that He might do it God's way. Even in death Jesus gives us an example of how to live and how to worship.

As for worship that is worthy of God and worthy of His people, James gives us further insight. In its crudest definition, worship can be said to be the paying of a compliment. If this is the case, what greater compliment can be paid than doing what someone asks? For James, there is no greater or more obvious form of worship than practical service.

Such service is not performed to impress God, or to make us worthy of His love. It is an act of thanksgiving, an act of worship, an expression of what is in our heart. It is not something that is reserved for special Christians. It is not for the elite regiment of believers, but for all that have a heart that is truly filled with worship. In this context it is not about a special ability or a particular calling, it is about a desire to be thankful for what God has made you and given you.

God does not choose some to have servant's feet, or others to have servant's hands. He desires that we all have a servant's heart. It is necessary because of the close relationship between service and worship. True service, like true worship begins in the heart. There is not one single ministry that God gives which is not given for the purpose of serving. We have seen that Jesus described Himself as the 'Good Shepherd', a Shepherd that served to the point that He would give His life for His sheep.

The man whose life and actions were endorsed by God, the man who was God's own Son, who performed miracles, healed the sick, overruled the laws of nature, cast out demons, took a towel and washed feet. Feet that would have been dirty from the dusty roads of a hot dry climate. To a man guided by his nose or his mind, such an action would be unthinkable. To Jesus it was an opportunity to serve and to exalt God's way of doing things. A simple way of worshipping God. The difference between a good deed and an act of worship is not the work of the hands, or the state of the mind, it is the intent of the heart.

To James, like Jesus, such service does not manifest itself as hardship but worship. Such an attitude of heart took one of the problems of first century life and made it an opportunity to worship God.

Caring for orphans and widows was a great problem at the time James wrote. There were no social services offered by local government offices, nor were there charitable trusts in place to help such people. So for many, begging was the only alternative to dying on the streets.

The Scriptures are full of commands to help such people as the poor and needy, highlighting the continuing theme that runs through the epistle, of obedience to God's Word. James is not bringing fresh revelation; he is reiterating an important principle.

If obedience is an act of worship, so is compassion for the needy. To obey is to follow Jesus, to show compassion is to be like Him. To imitate or copy someone is a tribute. Just as youngsters imitate their favourite singers or footballers, we should imitate Jesus. The desire of our heart should be to be like Him. This is one of the most simple forms of worship that exists.

Every one who desires to be a disciple of the Saviour is challenged by the call to be like Him. What does that mean, if it does not mean to imitate His motives and actions?

As we look at His life and work on earth, we cannot fail to notice the impact of His teaching and miracles upon the more vulnerable people of society. He taught that those who were healthy did not need a doctor. We are called to follow that example.

James with such a principle in mind makes a very important statement, the key to which is 'look after' or visit. It is not enough to make verbal commitments or recite platitudes. Nor is it enough to encourage others to help. It is not even enough to pay for others to help. All of these things are commendable, helpful and important, but they all fall short on their own. God desires that we visit the needy, where they are. James is doing no more than following the example of Jesus. God gave the Law to Moses, prophetic words to men like Isaiah and David and angelic visitations to others in preparation for the coming of the Messiah. Yet when it came to meeting the greatest need of man, He did not send the hosts of heaven, or even the highest of archangels, He came Himself, to where we were. He visited us in our need and met it. To do as Jesus did is our highest calling and true worship indeed. It is precious to God and worthy of Him.

To visit the needy and the vulnerable is to fulfil God's requirement for our lives. The Old Testament records the problems that Judah and Israel faced as a result of not understanding the message of God. It was not the sacrifices that God accepted as worship, but obedience to His Word. A Word that not only desired, but commanded compassion and kindness to the vulnerable. To God, standing up for the rights of the oppressed and the ignored was of greater importance than blind obedience to a sacrificial system that could not of itself bring salvation, but spoke of One that could. The One of which it spoke was Christ, the greatest champion of the downtrodden the world has ever seen.

We looked earlier at the temptation of David by Bathsheba, and learned an important lesson. In Psalm 51:16-17 we see another. David having realized what he had done, had repented before God and prays 'You do not delight in sacrifice, or I would bring it; you do not take pleasure in burnt offerings. The sacrifices of God are a broken spirit; a broken and contrite heart, O God, you will not despise.'

Isaiah was used greatly by God as a prophet during the time of the Old Testament. He was a man who recognized the

48

importance of this truth. He saw that helping the fatherless, the oppressed and widows, was a clear instruction from God. In Isaiah 1:17 he writes, 'Learn to do right! Seek justice, encourage the oppressed. Defend the cause of the fatherless, plead the case of the widow.' God does not make this optional; it is His expectation of us. Anything short will fail Him. To act according to such standards is more than obedience; it is worship. Worship that is worthy of Him.

We should also remember that such compassion to God's people is an act of worship because of the value God places upon the recognition of His people. Jesus taught in Matthew 25 that the simplest act of kindness shown to another would not go without its reward. The reward is not linked to the size of the deed, but to the desire to serve in a practical way. If a cup of cold water given to a thirsty man has its own reward, what of a toy given to an orphan or a cup of tea to the widow? To man such deeds are seen as acts of kindness, but to God they are seen as acts of worship. Maybe we should remind ourselves that the greatest man that ever walked this earth was homeless! Jesus had no home or possessions to call His own. How we treat such people, shows how we would have treated Him.

It is important that we recognize the people of God, not for what they are (i.e. imperfect), but for whose they are (i.e. God's). If you cannot see what Jesus sees in others, you will lose out on great blessing, but if you cannot see Him in others you will not see Him in your own life. That this is important is seen throughout the New Testament. Those who truly sought Him, when they found Him, they worshipped Him.

God has called us to worship Him with more than just our lips. He desires the worship of our whole heart, and therefore our actions. Such worship does not, cannot, and will not bypass the hands and the feet.

To James, true worship is more than a reflection of what is in the heart, it is a realization of it. What is in our heart takes the shape of reality in our actions.

Worship is not only about practical service, it is also about personal holiness. How we conduct ourselves is an important indicator of who we are, what we really believe, and how those beliefs affect us.

If being like Jesus is an act of worship, being holy must be conceived of as worship. To be holy is to be like Jesus. James links the standard of our speech and the manner of our life as being important, especially if we are to offer ourselves as objects of worship acceptable to God.

In line with this we are warned against self-deception. The man who is preoccupied with his own life is selfish, but the man who pays too little attention to himself is foolish and deceived if he considers his worship is acceptable to God. We are told constantly throughout the Scriptures that God is holy. This being the case, the first observation we can make and the first conclusion we can draw is that our worship must be holy. During the times of the Old Testament sacrifices, all offerings had to be set apart and pure. Second best was not good enough. Old or injured animals were not acceptable for sacrifices. This is a perfect example of what is acceptable to God today, and a perfect picture of worship of which He is worthy.

Holiness is not about a mystical or ethereal quality. It is about being separate from the world and set apart from its standards and values. We must be separated 'from' and set apart 'to'. One without the other is ineffective. It is not enough to be separate from the world and not be set apart to God. God does not desire to share our worship with another.

James informs us we must be separate from the world because of its polluting influence. Pure worship cannot proceed from a life that is polluted, just as pure water cannot flow from contaminated water sources.

The onus of responsibility lies with us. We are to keep ourselves from being affected by the world and its standards. Of course we need God's help, but the responsibility is ours. When James uses the word 'keep', he is using a word that is much stronger in meaning than is conveyed in the English language. Its primary meaning is not so much to retain as to watch over or guard. We must not take our conduct or actions for granted, we must watch over them. We cannot neither assume, nor presume that everything is acceptable. What God has planted in us and planned for us must be guarded as the most precious things we possess. The destiny we have in God is threatened when we do not guard ourselves, and allow God's protection to both permeate and dominate our lives.

We must protect ourselves against being influenced by evil. We cannot isolate ourselves from the world, and to attempt to do so would be wrong. Our calling is a dual one; to be in the world, but not of it. We are the lights of righteousness and holiness that shine in the darkness of our world.

I can remember back to my childhood when the United Kingdom was held in the grip of a strike. It was a difficult and emotive time, yet my recollections are not of the politics, but of the many power cuts and 'blackouts'. It was a time of candles, torches and oil lamps. One lesson I learned that is particularly appropriate to recall here is that oil lamps do not just need oil! They need the right type of oil. Clean, unadulterated and unpolluted oil. Oil that had been left in the shed for years and was contaminated with other things, did not burn, or did not burn cleanly.

We should not underestimate the power of pollution. During the last quarter of the twentieth century, man became painfully aware of the effects of pollution on the planet. Weather patterns, vegetation and animal life became adversely affected by climatic and environmental changes brought about by pollutants. The less subtle pollutants such as oil spills have had dramatic and obvious effects upon the ecology of the earth, while less obvious and more subtle pollutants have had equally damaging effects.

Within our lives and especially our worship, we must be on our guard against the obvious and the less obvious pollutants. Sin, whether obvious or subtle, ravages the lives of individuals, families, communities and even nations alike, more than any pollutant known to man could ever do.

We need to be aware that the enemy plans to corrupt our lives with evil. We need God's Word to constantly cleanse and wash us. It will prevent the filth of the world from sticking to and contaminating us.

We noted earlier one of the many important lessons Jesus taught His disciples. It involved a basin of water and a towel. In John 13 we read that He took the water and washed His disciples' feet, drying them with the towel. As on other occasions when Jesus was teaching, Peter adds his own thoughts on the matter. As a result of Peter's intrusion into the lesson we learn an important principle. The person who has bathed does not need to bath again immediately after, but he will need to wash his feet. Though he is clean, those parts of his body that touch the dirt and the dust of life will need to be washed again. Spiritually, though we are clean through the saving power of Jesus Christ, we need to ensure that our feet are continually brought into the presence of God and subjected to the power of His Word to cleanse. Such actions guard the holiness of life that is so vital as the fount of our worship to God.

God took it upon Himself to make it possible for us to be holy. Only we can choose it for ourselves. We will be as holy as we want to be. Maybe we will not be as holy as we may pretend, claim, or wish, but we will be as holy as we allow God to make us.

To understand God's desire for us and our lives is to understand the need to be holy. To understand the need to be holy is to be prepared to allow God to accomplish the task, whatever it takes.

Worship that is acceptable to God comes from a desire for holiness in how we think, speak, act and live. God's desire is that we live out what He has done in us. With this He is well pleased.

CHAPTER SIX

The Folly of Favouritism

My brothers, as believers in our glorious Lord Jesus Christ, don't show favouritism (James 2:1).

As James continues on with his epistle he brings to our attention a vitally important, but often ignored subject. The subject is prejudice and favouritism. Most people are raised to understand the importance of respect, and its place as a pillar of community life, but James is taking the principle to a greater than social context. He is taking it to a spiritual level.

James is now dealing with one of the biggest and potentially most serious blockages of blessing in a believer's life and the life of our churches. Unless we take heed to the warning James gives we will not see the fullness of the blessing of God on and in our lives. That is the degree of seriousness with which James approaches this subject.

The context in which James writes is an interesting one. We see from James 2:6 that he is not writing concerning what might happen, but rather what has already taken place. Prejudice and favouritism was already a part of some churches. This may come as a shock to those who think that the Early Church was perfect, it wasn't! The New Testament reflects the truth about the early Christians. There are few better pictures of the Early Church than is seen in Acts 6:1-7. There is a recognizing of the needs of the people, there is a desire and determination to meet them, but also there is evidence of prejudice and favouritism. If we consider that James was a leader in this church at Jerusalem, it may be that the events recorded in Acts 6 were at the forefront of his mind when he wrote his epistle.

We also see in this account that the strength of the New Testament Church is not the absence of faults but the determination to address them, even to the point of restructuring the leadership and the appointment of a new office. Discrimination had to be dealt with then and it needs to be dealt with now, even if church structures need to be altered to accommodate the solution.

That discrimination was not totally dealt with or understood is seen from the events recorded in Acts 10. What Peter receives from God is one of the greatest revelations that any man has received since the ascending of Jesus into heaven. Like many other Christians, Peter had discriminated against the Gentiles in his preaching of the Gospel message. The revelation that Peter receives teaches him that God looks upon all men as equal. Yet once Peter was convinced, others had to be convinced too. It was not really until the ministry of Paul that the good news of salvation was accepted as being equally for the Gentile as well as the Jew.

It is easy for us to look back and be critical of bygone generations, but there was great opportunity for discrimination in the first century. Men and women were not treated as equals, slavery was of vast proportions and the movement throughout the Roman World of people of differing nationalities was great. Wherever they could be found, Jews, Greeks and Romans alike endeavoured to uphold their own traditions and favoured their own people. Such things as creed, colour, wealth, circumstance of birth, sex, education and ability separated people. The Gospel of Jesus Christ was to be instrumental then and throughout history as a barrier breaker.

The relevance of such a topic should not be lost upon us. For though fantastic changes have taken place in the last two thousand years, bias and prejudice are still very much a part of life.

One of the first holidays that my wife and I took after we were married was in a beautiful coastal resort in Wales. At the rear of the flat that we rented was a bowling green, where visitors could try their hand at the noble summer pastime. Being a keen sportsman and competitive by nature, I tried everything I knew in order to win, but the harder I tried the worse I became. Others made the game look easy; I made it look impossible. Though the problem was simple, the solution was beyond my ability. I could not control the bias that existed within the bowl.

There is a bias within each of us. We all feel more comfortable in surroundings we know and among people with whom we naturally relate or share common interests. It is not wrong to relate more easily to some than to others.

Preference is not the same as partiality. The issue is not about where we feel most comfortable. It is not about whether we are proud of our upbringing or even ashamed of our roots. This is about why we draw the conclusions that we do. If there is within us a bias concerning wealth or poverty, race or nationality, we must learn to deal with the bias. Failure to do so will be costly in that it could cost us our destiny.

The significance of this issue may be further seen from the bloodstained pages of history. Pages stained with the blood of innocents, for which someone will have to answer. Sectarian wars between factions and nations, civil disorder, rioting, acts of terrorism and reprisals, acts of brutality wrongly dignified by the title of religious war, haunt the history books of many countries.

The source of such conflict does not stem from a healthy understanding of history, but an unhealthy lack of understanding of the danger of discrimination.

National identity or cultural influence is not something to be ashamed of, nor should it be denied its rightful place. However, failure to remember that the whole of the earth was in existence before our forefathers walked the land of our birth, and that it was and is God's, is not ignorance but negligence. Negligence in not thinking through the equality of all nations as the creation of God.

The world in which we live is rife with favouritism and discrimination, and each and every society has its own forms of the manifestations of this sin. If it infiltrates the Church we cease to stand for what God has called us to stand. Paul, one of the greatest influences upon first century Christianity wrote in Galatians 3:28 'There is neither Jew nor Greek, slave nor free, male nor female, for you are all one in Christ Jesus.' The whole basis of the ministry of the man who became known as the 'Apostle to the Gentiles' was built upon this understanding of the non-discriminatory and impartial love of God for all men.

The man whose life has been touched by God will be recognizable because he will be a man whose heart does not judge or draw conclusions based upon discriminatory factors.

We have been warned to keep ourselves away from polluting influences; few leave a smell as obnoxious as discrimination. We must heed the warning James gives to us and guard against it at all costs.

To show favouritism is to live in the natural, not in the spiritual. James gives an example of a wrong attitude; an attitude that manifests itself, like all wrong attitudes, in wrong behaviour.

Whether the example given is something that James had seen in Jerusalem, heard related from elsewhere or is purely hypothetical, we do not know, but we do know the point that James is teaching; the folly of discrimination.

We are told of two men from very different backgrounds receiving two very different forms of treatment from the same people. The rich man in James 2:2 is said to possess a gold ring. It is likely that this would have signified that he was a holder of a political or social office of some importance. However important the office he held, it does not signify he is of more importance or less importance than any other human being in the eyes of God. The judgement giving this man preferential treatment over another is not based on spiritual values, but natural.

We all have the right to choose our friends and decide the basis of those choices for ourselves. We have the right, but we also have the responsibility of accounting for the way that we treat all human beings. We must not forget that all men are made in the image of God. We need to arrive at decisions based upon spiritual values.

Why did these believers give preferential treatment to a rich man over a poor man? The answer needs to be carefully thought out in light of the issue of partiality. Firstly it is not a criticism of the rich man and his wealth or position, which though a subject in itself, is not the issue here. It is not even the way that the rich man is treated that is wrong, rather it is that the poor man was not given the same treatment that is at fault. The partiality that was shown reveals a number of things.

Firstly the treatment given suggests that those judging did not see both men as God saw them. The judgement is seen as based upon appearance, but God does not judge by outward appearance, but by the heart. He is not fickle and shallow as are those who make such judgements. A man may have new clothes today, but in ten years' time he could be wearing the same clothes. Now they are rags, does it make him less of the image of God? Does it make him of less value or worth to God? Does it now mean Jesus would not have died for him?

Jesus treated all men according to the same principles, faith and need. When Jesus saw the needs of people He dealt with them on a first come first met basis, not on a best-dressed or highest worth basis. Jesus ministered according to need. When the hungry were before Him, He fed them. When the sick were before Him, He healed them. To those prepared to receive and exercise faith He took the time to honour that faith and wrought miracles within their lives. He did not look for character references or qualifications. Faith and need were enough.

Now we must delve further below the surface. What causes a man to judge or discriminate in such a way? There is a very real danger that churches and Christians lose sight of their calling. Our calling is to service not respectability. If we are looking to 'belong' here and be a part of the world we will seek to ingratiate ourselves with the wealthy, the worldly, the powerful and influential. We will look to be a part of their social circle and share in their allegiances.

Our place at the table of life is to serve, not to be served. There is a further danger that we seek to meet the needs of society by impressing them rather than ministering to them. Some look to the rich and famous to endorse their Christianity, to give credence to their beliefs. There has been a tendency to use stars from the world of sport or entertainment to give such credibility to Christianity. We should remember that while it is right that celebrities publicly testify for Jesus, credibility is not ours or theirs to give, only God's. Only He can give credibility to Christianity. Only He can give the life and power to live as a Christian. If what Jesus thinks of us and of others alike is not a guiding influence in how we live, we need to repent, reread the Gospels and start again.

We should be careful that we do not fall into the trap of seeking the world's approval to avoid persecution. We must accept opposition as part of the cross that we are called to bear. This should not cause us to seek compromise with the world, but rather to rejoice that we are found worthy to suffer for the name of Jesus. If we suffer for Him and with Him, we shall reign with Him too.

There is possibly a sense in which many are afraid to identify with the needy. In Luke 10 we read the Parable of the Good Samaritan. We admire the hero of the story for his bravery, helping the wounded man at the risk of his own life. We are not told what he felt or if he was afraid, only what he did. He was not the first on the scene, but he was the first to make a difference. Our calling and destiny does not depend on how we feel, or who gets there first, but whether we make a difference when confronted by a need.

The priest and Levite were prejudiced. They put other people, themselves and other things before a man in need. The irony that Jesus gives is that it was a Samaritan who helped. A man from among a people often discriminated against. The priest and Levite came from a background rife with favouritism and discrimination. In the case of the man in need on the Jerusalem to Jericho road, they could no longer make decisions that were fair and impartial. That is what prejudice does. It affects everything you do and every decision you make.

For some to be seen with the needy will cause embarrassment in their social circle. If that is the case, a real problem is emerging. The criticism that echoed in the ears of Jesus was that He was a friend of sinners. Unless we are prepared to carry that particular cross we will never be like Jesus.

We have to be very careful that our minds have not been twisted by the values of this world. We are taught in the affluent West that poverty is a terrible thing, and with much of the world living under the effects of poverty it is not a subject that should be taken lightly. Jesus had much to say about both poverty and riches. In Mark 8:36 we see one of the most quoted verses in the Bible, 'What good is it for a man to gain the whole world, yet forfeit his soul?' It is better to be a child of God and poor, than rich without Him. Jesus, not only identified with the poor, He became poor. In 2 Corinthians 8:9 Paul reminds us that the reason Jesus became poor was that we might share in His riches. If you want to judge wealth, judge it by spiritual values. If you want to grow spiritually, surround yourselves with those who possess spiritual riches. What they impart to you will outlast time.

To despise the poor is to despise Jesus. To insult the poor, which James accuses them of doing, is to insult Jesus also. To be great in the eyes of God will be to be like Jesus. What He had He gave up for others. God does not judge by what you receive, but what you retain.

The early Christians sold what they had and gave to the poor. God rewards, blesses and exalts those who see the poor, not as an embarrassment but as an opportunity to shine as the light of the world.

We have been preoccupied with the example of wealth and position but they are by no means exclusively the only areas where prejudice and favouritism raise their ugly head. We must accept no barriers.

There are sadly those who will not listen to or will not take instruction from women who minister or prophesy. There are similar people who judge a person by their age rather than by God's anointing. For others, lack of formal training or education in a minister is seen as reason for not listening or heeding to what he may have to say. As unrealistic as some of these may sound, they are examples that may be found to be true. Too often we judge by what man sets as a standard, not God.

None of the prejudices we have are biblical in their foundation, yet they exist. I am certain of God's love for me, that He has a plan for my life, but He does not seek my consent when He gives out His anointing. It is my responsibility to receive from such as are anointed to teach and preach by His Spirit. There is a thin line, between a 'spiritual arrogance' that dictates to God who is acceptable for anointing, and a denial of whom God has anointed. The former grieves the Holy Spirit, but the latter is extremely closely bordering on blasphemy. It is a line so thin that mostly it is not visible. Opposition to God's anointed is opposition to God. To give such opposition is a serious and grievous offence in the eyes of God.

We must also learn from the instruction James gives that to show favouritism is to fail to identify with God. A true Christian cannot help but be seen by others to be a follower of Jesus. An important spiritual principle that should hallmark every believer's life is that light always shines in darkness. In our conversation, our attitude, our values and our actions, people must always identify us with God. Whether we are identifying with His people or with His Word, people must always see us identifying with Him.

This is light shining in darkness. Jesus Christ indwelling us by His Spirit is the only value we have to show the world. It is the part of us that glows in the darkness. If we are not identifying ourselves with God, we are snuffing out the very light that should be shining.

To identify with Him is to identify with His ways, opinions, standards and statements. Also it is important we identify with those He has chosen. Often, James points out, it is those who are poor in the eyes of the world that God chooses to be heirs of salvation. Yet such people are mistreated at the hands of those who cause believers so many problems. James is concerned that his readers are turning their backs on those with whom God has chosen to identify Himself.

There is a popular saying that describes the people James is writing about, 'they run with the hare and hunt with the hounds'. The Christian cannot do such a thing. He has to decide which master he will follow and serve. To be a Christian you have to identify yourself with Christ. To identify yourself with Christ you have to identify yourself with His people.

It is both an awful and a sinful thing to side with those who oppose Christ and the people He has chosen to call His own. I am sure we can all recall times when Christians have sided with unbelievers in criticizing the Church and other Christians. To do so is to fall into a dangerous error. Whatever we may think of a particular Christian or group of Christians, we do not have licence to judge others. We must be very careful in what we say about other believers, and equally as careful of how we say it, when we say it and where we say it. There is a danger that criticizing God's children becomes a criticism of God.

We have already seen the example of Jesus in siding with the poor and the oppressed. We should also note the bias in the ministry that God gives is to the lost, the ill, the needy and the vulnerable. If we are to be ministers of salvation, healing, power and blessing, to whom can we minister, if not to those who need such things?

To minister with partiality is to deny Jesus, and the power of His Gospel; a Gospel that opposes the oppressor, and seeks to help the oppressed.

In Luke 4 we see the account of Jesus being tempted by the devil and His visit to the synagogue at Nazareth. He is offered riches and rule by the devil, but resists the temptation. Compare what He was offered during the temptation with what He chose. Taking the scroll of the prophet Isaiah, He reads from the sixty-first chapter, making an important pronouncement. That pronouncement sets and describes the nature of His ministry. He is anointed by God to minister to the poor, imprisoned, blind and oppressed. He is to show God's favour to them and meet their needs. This is the man who turned His back on the temptation of riches and rule and chose to help the needy and socially unimportant. Why? Because it was what the Father had asked Him to do.

This is not about bank balances and building society

accounts, but the futility of self-reliance and the importance of faith. Jesus was never at home with those whose dependence was on themselves, their possessions and abilities. Yet when He was among social outcasts and those despised in the eyes of others (people who did not trust in themselves, but God) He was clearly where He wanted to be. The question that now raises itself is, 'How much like Jesus are we?'

As a result of the challenge James places before us we should consider the thoughts and the motives on which we build our relationships, our friendships, our hopes, our ambitions, our speech and our actions. Ungodly and unholy alliances have cost many lost blessings and unfulfilled destinies. The teaching of the New Testament is totally clear on this subject. Friendship with and love of the world, its standards, its possessions and positions is opposed to God. If our love for God is not above all and every part of the world, we will show partiality and favouritism.

There are many instances and examples of occasions when a word or action can place us in a position that can compromise our identification with God. We must do everything we can through holy living to avoid such situations, but should they still arise we must stand and be counted, confronting and dealing with the situation as befitting a child of God. If we are not for Him, we are against Him. If we are not for His people, it is not His people we are against, but Him.

James takes this subject yet another step further. To show favouritism is to disobey the royal law of God. This is a challenge to all that would claim to keep the royal law of God. Many people seem to think that you judge a Christian by what he does not do. This is not so. Obedience is rarely proven by what we do not do, but by what we actually do. Because a person refrains from a particular thing proves little. What he replaces it with does! A person may not use bad language. It proves self-

THE FOLLY OF FAVOURITISM

control, but on its own no more than that. To not use bad language is admirable, but to be a gossip or rumour-monger is to be no different than a person who uses filthy language. The test is not what you do not say, but what you do say!

Obedience to God's royal law can only be proven by what we do. We must love without partiality, without favouritism and without judgement. God loves unconditionally; this is His desire and expectancy of us.

Those who keep God's law keep His royal law. James picks out the commandment in Leviticus 19:18 that we should love our neighbour as ourselves, as being special. In Matthew 22:34-40 Jesus describes this commandment and the commandment to love God with every part of our being as the foundation on which all other requirements of the Christian life are built. To love without partiality is a royal law for it was given assent by the King of kings. To Jesus it was the very embodiment of the challenge that He would lay at the feet of the first Christians. In John 15:9 we read words from one of the Saviour's most deeply profound discourses, 'As the Father has loved me, so have I loved you. Now remain in my love.' This was not the end of what Jesus had to say about love but rather the beginning. In verse 12 we see Him lay down a challenge in the form of a commandment, 'My command is this: Love each other as I have loved you.'

If we are to love as Jesus loved, how are we to love? Perfectly, without partiality or preference based upon natural reason or logic; without an expectation of personal gain or advancement as a result of our love. This is the basis on which we are to love our neighbour.

We should further consider here the relevance of the call to love our neighbour. They are usually random. We do not usually choose them. When a person moves house it is only occasionally because they want to live near their new neighbours. It is usually for one of a host of other reasons. To love our neighbour as the Bible teaches is a great test of our impartiality.

James makes it abundantly clear that this is a vitally important issue for it strikes right at the heart of our Christianity. To love with partiality is to be guilty of breaking the law of God.

There is a grave danger that we weight each commandment with degrees of severity. Unfortunately we usually weight them as the world sees them. As a result, adultery and murder are bad, while loving with partiality and gossiping are considered only minor offences. James makes it as clear as he possibly can that this could not be further from the truth. To break the law of God is to break the law of God! There are no degrees of sin in God's eyes. There is no sin so slight that it does not require the death of Jesus to atone for it. To show favouritism is no less in God's eyes than murder or adultery. It is just that it is easier for us to disguise, excuse and sweep under the carpet. It is not so with God.

As if James had not stressed the importance of impartiality enough, he goes even further again. To judge without mercy is to invite judgement without mercy on ourselves. We will see elsewhere in the epistle the importance of sowing and reaping, but here its application is obvious. If we do not sow in mercy we will not reap mercy. Worse still, in judging without mercy we are denying the existence of mercy in our own lives, and also its effects. To live without mercy, is to live under the power and effects of sin. If our lives are an image of Jesus, we must reflect mercy in all our dealings with the people among whom we live and with whom we come into contact.

We are often too focused on why we are not blessed, rather than why we are not a blessing to others. If we focused on the latter we would see the issues that cause a lack of blessing in our own lives. Merciless judgement lives right at the core of favouritism and prevents blessing accordingly. The quickest way to stop blessing in our own lives is to stop being in a position to bless others.

The Christian whose life is centred on Jesus is free from partiality and favouritism. He sees others, as Christ first saw him.

CHAPTER SEVEN

Fruitful Faith

As the body without the spirit is dead, so faith without deeds is dead (James 2:26).

The subject of faith is an emotive one for many believers and unbelievers alike. Throughout the history of the Church few subjects have been as hotly debated as this one, with James 2:14-26 at the centre of the debate. Such is the strength of feeling that some notable theologians have doubted the very validity of this epistle. Such doubt is the result of failing to understand the passage in question and the relevance of its context.

It is not our ability to debate that is called into question here, nor is it our understanding of theology, but our ability to interpret the Scriptures correctly. Before we start comparing the sermons of Jesus with the writings of James and Paul we need to consider how we should interpret Scripture. It is not enough to compare Scripture with Scripture. We must make such a comparison based on each Scripture being in its correct context. Every verse must be seen in the context of its setting, and the purpose of its writer in including it in such a setting.

The primary purpose of James in writing was not to produce a commentary on the writing of another, but to convey a message of his own. The same can be said of all the other writings of the New Testament. Each was written in its own context and setting. Understanding this context and setting is the key to unlocking many misunderstandings and errors. Until we understand the place of a statement in a particular epistle, we cannot understand the wider implications of its inclusion in the New Testament.

James is stressing throughout this epistle the importance of fruit in the life of a believer. He is looking at the journey a believer makes after accepting salvation by faith. Once we understand this, we see that there is no conflict between James and the teaching of either Jesus or Paul.

In Matthew 7:16 Jesus instructs His followers to look at a person and recognize the validity of their contribution by their fruit. It is true that speech can give an indication of a person's thoughts and motives, but the overall fruit they produce is a much more certain indicator. This may be contrary to what some Christians understand. There was a popular saying during my time at Bible College, 'It's not by their suits, but by their fruits' that we recognize a person's ministry. Appearance does not count for the same as fruit. Paul and James alike recognized this point and encouraged people to active Christianity, warning of the consequences of failing in this. Actions matter greatly.

Spiritual principles are always appropriate markers by which we may interpret the Scriptures and fruit is one of the fundamental principles of Christian living. The Bible teaches that everything that possesses life bears fruit, while everything that is dead does not. Further to this we are taught that the type of fruit produced is determined by the nature of its producer. Creation reproduces after its kind. This is one of the earliest lessons that God taught mankind. Grapes grow only on vines. Vines produce after their kind. The animal kingdom is exactly the same, and the spiritual realm is no different. Faith in keeping with this principle produces fruit after its own kind.

If we take the issue of faith as Paul teaches it, in the context he teaches, and do the same with James, we will discover that rather than have a contradiction, what we have is a fuller picture than if we take each on their own. This is one of the special qualities of Scripture. Comments made to those who believe good works will earn them salvation will always seem to be at odds with comments made to those who believe that confession, but no fruit, is acceptable Christian living. Left is the same as right to men facing in opposite directions.

We must understand the context of which James writes, for it is absolutely essential we practice 'faith living' in our Christian lives. Living by faith is not optional for the Christian; it is the normal way of living. If we do not understand it, it is unlikely that we live by it.

As James writes so strongly and so passionately concerning the way believers live, and the centrality of faith to such a life, it is no surprise that he approaches the subject with an unswerving determination to stress the point. It is a subject that we should share with such a passion.

Perhaps before we examine faith we should be sure of what it is not. James 2:14 tells us that the initial context is not faith, but the claim to have faith. Like James we have the right to observe and draw conclusions from what we see. This is not judging, merely observing and learning.

If you were sold a tree and told that it was a pear tree, how would you know it was what it was claimed to be? Maybe you would be able to identify it by the shape or colour of the leaves, the shape of the branches or even the shape of the tree itself. The ultimate test or proof would be the fruit. It could pass for a pear tree but if it produced apples, it would not be a pear tree. In an age of genetic engineering we should remember not to try and tamper with the laws and principles of the Kingdom of God.

Faith in the sense the Bible speaks of does not exist because someone says it does. Many like the person in James 2:14 claim to have faith when they do not. Faith is not a confession or a statement. It is something that is real and tangible. In Hebrews

11:1 we see that faith is more than words, it is even more than hope. It is the reason for, and the embodiment of hope. Hope without faith is at best positive thinking and at worst wishful thinking. Neither produces the fruit of faith. With faith, hope becomes the basis on which we look to the future; something in which we can invest our lives.

Without hope, in this context, we have nothing of real value to look forward to or live by. The man who confesses to have with his lips, what he does not have in his heart, is at best ignorant of the meaning of faith and at worst deceived or a deceiver. Yet such people exist. They were around when James was writing and they are around today.

We must heed the warning that faith is not positive thinking. There are those who believe that if they think long enough and hard enough, and claim verbally whatever it is they claim to believe, it will come to pass. Faith is not merely saying God heals, it is a belief, based upon God's Word, that He heals.

A positive attitude to life should accompany every believer, but however positive my state of mind may be, it does not heal the sick, or cause miracles to take place. Only God can perform such miracles, but He acts in response to faith, not positive thinking. Saying that Jesus has saved me or wishing I was saved is not the same as believing I am saved through faith in Jesus Christ.

James goes further in his description of what faith is not. In James 2:19 we see that it is neither a mental understanding nor a mental appreciation. It is neither learned facts nor knowledge gained through observation. Evil spirits know that God exists. They even understand aspects of His being, and certainly need no convincing of His power and authority, yet they do not live by faith. Trembling before God, or even fear of His greatness does not amount to faith.

It would appear from the way James writes and the specific

nature of his arguments that he has a certain person or group of people in mind. There may be intellectual understanding, even a mental assent, but no faith.

University life taught me many things about human nature and life. It also taught me spiritual principles. I learned that there was more to Christianity than theology. There appeared to be a clear divide between the people with whom I spent most of my time. There were those who trusted in learning, in knowledge and in the gaining of information. Such people's lives are only touched in as much as there is a sense of satisfaction from the process of learning itself. Yet while knowledge influences decisions, it rarely changes lives; nor does it, of itself, bring a deeper relationship with God. The other group was equally intelligent, but lived not by intelligence but by faith. Their spare time was filled with evangelism, praying for the sick and having fellowship together. They finished the day with faith that thrilled their souls rather than facts that just stimulated their minds. It was a faith that drew them into a closer relationship with God. They saw dramatic things take place; things that do not result from intellectual appraisals but from faith. Their lives were marked out, not by what they knew but whom they knew. Their lives were a living testimony to a living faith in a living God.

Understanding the doctrine of healing is good and important, but alone it will not heal the sick; that comes through faith in God. Understanding is only of value when it is mixed with faith in order to produce fruit.

There is still another aspect of what faith is not. It is not good works! There exists a deceptive fallacy that believes that to be a Christian is to be a 'do-gooder'. If we read carefully the words of James 2:14-26 we will notice that James goes to great lengths to emphasize the relationship between faith and works. Works without faith are of no value.

FRUITFUL FAITH

The illustration of Abraham shows this clearly. Had he not believed God, would he have been described as 'God's friend' and would his actions have been credited to him as righteousness? The answer is clearly no. There is no confusion here between James and Paul. The latter teaches clearly that it is not possible to appear righteous before God by human effort alone. James is not disputing the necessity of faith to please God, nor do his writings dispute the necessity of faith for salvation. He seeks to define the difference between living faith and dead faith. He also establishes the importance of works as evidences of faith, not faith's alternative.

If as James confirms, faith and works coexist, they are of necessity different. To deny the need for faith as separate to good works is to totally miss the point that James is making so forcefully.

The faith that truly saves is a living faith. This is the starting point of understanding the meaning of faith, and the stepping stone to distinguishing it from dead faith.

To illustrate this point let us take the example of a battery. The definition of a battery is 'a cell or series of cells that produce electricity'. Central to its definition and function is that it produces electricity. What of a battery that does not produce electricity? Is it now a battery, or merely a metal object? For the sake of convenience a dead battery is still referred to as a battery, though its function, or lack of it, really defines it as something else. If I were to collect a load of dead batteries and sell them as batteries, I would probably be breaking the law. What then of faith? Just as with a dead battery, dead faith is faith in name, not in nature. If it is not alive, it is not faith. In the absence of another word to describe it, we misleadingly still refer to it as faith.

If we are to understand the faith that both James and Paul write about, we must appreciate that it is life changing and real.

73

It is not theoretical or hypothetical. It is a faith that is at the centre of their beliefs, actions and motivations. It is alive.

We know from Ephesians 2:8 that faith is given by God, and God doesn't give dead gifts, He deals in life. Every gift we receive from His hand is given that we might grow and mature in our spiritual lives. Jesus came as the life giver. It is inconsistent then to think that any gift that God gives would be anything other than living.

Such faith as James describes must be living, for only the living can change things. Faith in Jesus alters attitudes, changes hearts, heals bodies and saves souls with a frequency and magnitude beyond our understanding. This is not a dead and lifeless ritualistic belief, but living and vibrant faith.

We are now touching on the central point of faith. We have already noted the spiritual principle that all living things produce fruit, a point at the very core of understanding faith. Not all plants produce beautiful flowers or edible leaves or stems, but they do all have an effect on their immediate environment. In some cases the effect may be minor, but the effect still exists. For us as Christians, our speech, actions, motivation, hopes and ambitions all contribute to the effect, whether positive or negative, we have on the environment around us.

If we reread James 2:14-26 and exchange the words signifying deeds or works for the word fruit the passage becomes much clearer. James is challenging the notion that faith can exist without producing fruit. Remember the battery! Dead faith produces no fruit, so if there is no fruit the faith in question must be dead.

True faith produces the kind of fruit that identifies the 'tree' as belonging to God. Remember that it was Jesus who warned that fruit was the identifying evidence we should look for in a believer's life. A spiritual man produces spiritual fruit.

A man may claim to have faith and not have it. The man who does have it will be clearly visible because the faith he has will produce the fruit of faith. This is the emergence of the principle of like gives birth to like. Faith comes from God, therefore it will produce fruit in line with the life of Jesus; hence the example given by James. To offer words to a man who is hungry and cold, without meeting the obvious need is not the fruit that faith in Jesus produces.

In 1 John 3:17 we are told that if the love of God dwells within us, it will shine out of us by helping such people as James uses to illustrate his point. Fruit is a reflection of what is in the tree. Good trees do not produce bad fruit and vice versa.

Jesus did not offer platitudes to the poor and needy, He met their needs. He did not offer sympathy to the sick, but went to where they were and healed them. These actions are the fruit of a good tree; they are the fruit of faith.

A hallmark of the life of Jesus was obedience. This is one of the clearest evidences of the presence of faith. Note how the blessing and favour of God on the life of Abraham coincides with a life of obedience. Living faith is belief in action. This is seen in the examples James gives. Both Abraham's willingness to offer Isaac as a sacrifice and Rahab's willingness to help the spies are evidences of the faith they possessed. These were not the outcome of some deeply considered and studiously approached decisions but the fruit of faith.

Paul tells us in Ephesians 2:8-9 that works do not save us. James tells us that only living faith is of value. The man that has faith that brings salvation will have a faith that produces the appropriate fruit. In John 15 Jesus teaches another aspect to the principle of fruit bearing. He is the Vine, if we live in Him and follow His teaching, we will produce much fruit, but if we don't we will wither and die. Dead branches do not produce fruit; hence they get broken off and thrown in the fire. They hinder the plant's growth and are unsightly, that is why they are removed.

Great is the gift of faith that we receive from God for our salvation. Mighty is His grace and mercy in making us a part of His Vine. Serious is the responsibility we have to abide in the Vine. Unless we do our faith will die.

As we look at the fruit of faith we must be certain that our lives are founded upon the first and most important fruit, salvation. We must have the assurance that our lives are built upon faith in Jesus Christ rather than hope in our own endeavours. God looked upon Abraham's faith and credited it to him as righteousness and justification. Any and all of his failings and sins were forgiven because the faith he had in God was real and living. The proof of this is seen in the fruit his faith bore in his life. Our salvation must be based upon faith in Jesus. One of the fruits of such faith will be the assurance we are saved. Doubt, as we have already seen, is a fruit of human thinking, not of faith.

The fruit of faith begins at salvation, but it does not end there. James highlights a number of other aspects, all of which should be evident to every Christian. Evident not only in their thinking, but in their lives too.

Faith takes us beyond our natural understanding. We have seen that faith is not intellectual understanding, but we should also recognize that there is a major difference between the two. Intellect is limited. We are told by scientists that the brain of a human is not used to anywhere near its full potential, yet knowledge is limited to what we have learned, how much we are able to remember and how much of it is meaningful. There are obvious and great limitations. Faith is limitless. It knows no boundaries, for its strength is not in itself, but in Jesus, the One in whom it is placed.

There are those who have knowledge of spiritual things but

no faith. They live a life that is spiritually limited and therefore unfulfilled. Faith enlarges our lives with its greatness. We have already seen that to be blessed is to be enlarged, and faith with its infinite possibilities enlarges our expectation, our quality of life and our activities.

We are no longer bound by what our minds and our bodies tell us are our limits, or even by what other people say we can or cannot do. The laws of nature, of medicine and even of reason are no longer barriers to us. Faith causes us to know and to do the impossible.

James also shows that faith makes our witness to the world a valid one. If there is one criticism that is often made of the Church that ought not to be true, it must be that the Church sets a poor image of the Christian life. The fruit of faith clearly demonstrates to all that are able to see, what is the true nature of Christianity. This is the normal Christian life, the real Christian life; not the poor example set by those who claim to have faith but do not.

What greater example of the love of God can there be than the fruit of faith in a believer? Feeding the hungry, visiting the lonely, comforting the bereaved all point to the love of God, and the evidence of faith. This is the light that we are called to shine into darkness. This is not a learned or rehearsed process but the reality of fruit bearing faith.

Under legalism the keeping of the commandments is based upon personal actions. What we do becomes the measure of our lives. The change under Grace may appear to be subtle but it is great, for what we do does not make us what we are, but reflects what we already have become in Christ. This is not the doing of good works, but the bearing of fruit. Good works are a testimony to man and his efforts, but fruit is a testimony to God. Fruit bears witness to the tree, not to itself.

The fruit of faith does not testify to the world that a person has turned over a new leaf, as does good works, but it signals a new life. Not a change of mind, but a change of heart. It testifies of the One responsible for the change.

We see too that faith takes the promise of God and turns it into blessing. All Christians are the recipients of the promises of God, but not all receive the blessing those promises offer. The reason why is not to be found in the promise but in the need of faith to claim the promise and its blessing for ourselves.

Abraham received blessing because the fruit of his faith was more important than the fruit of his body. What a beautifully clear picture of the difference between faith and good works this story presents. Abraham believed God when He promised him that he would be the father of multitudes. The fruit of his faith was his willingness to sacrifice his only son Isaac. Though he was old, he knew that the promise of God was more reliant upon God than it was upon either the life of his son or the improbability of his old and tired body producing another son. Abraham would prove his faith by obeying God. To Abraham, faith was not a problem but a source of blessing.

Faith takes trials and promises alike and sees the blessing of God poured out upon our lives, and the lives of those around us. Whatever the circumstances, the fruit of faith is victory. This is not because it is the nature of faith, but because it is the nature of the One in whom our faith is placed.

CHAPTER EIGHT

Sanctified Speech

. . . If anyone is never at fault in what he says, he is a perfect man, able to keep his whole body in check (James 3:2).

James initially issues a challenge to would-be leaders, but goes on to develop a challenge relevant to all Christians. It is inevitable that those whose destiny will take them to positions of influence over other Christians must live by a higher standard; as the expectancy of them is greater, so must be the standards by which they live. To those who have been given greater gifts and talents, greater things are expected.

As James presents this to his readers, he addresses an issue that is vital to Christian living, the nature of our conversation. Is it not strange that with all the things Jesus did, and the way He lived, people still noticed and commented on the way He spoke?

We talk about the need in our churches of men who can perform the miraculous, and rightly so, but what about the need of men whose conversation and speech cause others to take notice and reflect that they have been with Jesus? Men in control of what they say and how they say it are an asset to their generation. We often look for the spectacular, but God looks for the sanctified.

There are many ways that we as individuals fail God, yet the subject highlighted by James is not only one of the most common ways, but one of the most far-reaching. Such is the emphasis that James wishes to place upon the matter that he is prepared to go as far as pointing out that the man who has tamed the tongue is a perfect man. In our search for perfection in the way we live, ought we not therefore to give considerable thought to the way we speak?

To many people in the world today, words are cheap. Many have become so used to being lied to and misled that they have become distrustful of what they hear. Lies are accepted as a part of life.

I attended a course for management training while working in the electronics industry in the 1980s. During one of the seminars the subject of truthfulness was raised, and what ensued surprised me greatly. When asked if lying was an acceptable practice for a manager, with the exception of three people, all of whom were Christians, everyone in the room, including the tutor, believed that it was.

If speech is cheap to many in western society, it certainly wasn't in first century Jewish culture. Remembering that this epistle was addressed primarily to Jewish Christians we should understand that words were thought to possess great power. Once spoken they could never be returned. They were thought to exist forever as a testimony of a man's heart.

James, understanding fully the implications of Jewish culture, seeks to press the Christian view of the subject of speech and words. Having stressed the importance of actions over speech, James now stresses the importance of speech. His teaching has at no point looked upon speech as unimportant. Rather he has looked for lives to be consistent, for speech and actions to testify of each other's validity.

Here James builds upon the same principles as in other subjects. The importance of speech is seen in that it is a reflection of our spiritual condition. If our actions should be consistent with our beliefs, so should our speech. We have already seen how favouritism makes our actions inconsistent, now we see that lack of control over the tongue leaves our speech inconsistent. If it is true that actions speak louder than words, it is not true to say that words have nothing to say at all. Nor is it true to say that because the fruit of our life is the greatest test of our Christianity, that what we say and how we say it is unimportant. Speech is a fruit of our lives. What James has been saying is that it is not the only fruit; not that it is not a fruit at all. The balanced Christian understands this, and also understands the dangers of inconsistency between words and deeds.

Those who have the greatest problems understanding the subjects James writes about, are those starting from preconceived standpoints, and those looking for wood to fuel argument and debate. The truth is that his epistle is written not for the theorist or the discusser of theology, but for those whose desire is to be like Jesus in everything they do. Such people will not strain at one aspect or another, but wholeheartedly embrace the truth of which James writes, in pursuit of holiness and the fulfilment of their destiny in God.

Of all the ways and means available to man to fail in his duty and responsibility to God, one of the easiest and most common must be through what he says. For James it is no less than an indicator of the level of completeness of a man's perfection and holiness. If a man's speech is holy, his whole being is holy, and if there is evil in the body, the tongue will reveal it.

The spiritual man will recognize the danger of the tongue and act to control it. He will not underestimate the danger of compromising speech, unholy conversation or language that does not edify or encourage.

Such is the power of the tongue that though man can tame the animals, he cannot control his tongue. This seems at first a slightly exaggerated comparison, but it has a true and deeper meaning. In Genesis 1:26 we read that the gift of God to man was dominion over the animals. Power and authority over the animal kingdom was to come to Adam's offspring, it was to be their right to rule. That relates to the natural world. Control over the tongue relates to the spiritual world. Only the offspring of God can know dominion over and control of the tongue.

If a man is living on the natural level, evil speech will be the result. He will not be able to control his tongue. It will become a vessel of dishonour. He may not blaspheme or swear, but control of the tongue comes only to those whose very life is controlled by God. We all like to think that we have control over this small, but influential part of the body, but the truth is we do not. Only God can give us the control we both desire and need.

There are Christians who mistakenly think that there is a middle ground between those who are spiritual and those who are natural in their outlook. This middle ground is where the nice and the good live. The religiously eccentric live at one extreme and the outwardly worldly and indifferent at the other. They, the good and the balanced live in the middle. Unfortunately for them this is not true.

There are only two relevant levels of existence in this context; the one where we are led by the Spirit of God and the one where we are not. Nowhere is this point better illustrated than here, in the subject of speech. The natural man, however disciplined and admirable his life, is not controlled by the Spirit of God and therefore his tongue will reflect the potential for evil.

In the illustration of the bit that is used to control the horse, there is an important point emphasized. The tongue or speech that is out of control assumes control of the whole. The mouth of the horse guides the horse. The horse, though tremendously strong, able to pull heavy loads, jump great heights and run at great speed, is controlled by his mouth.

James shows how applicable this is to the man making great

boasts. His life is governed by what he says. He has to live according to what he boasts and not necessarily to what he thinks or wants. This is only true of the man who is controlled by his mouth; it is not true of the man whose tongue is under control. It must not be the mouth that controls the man, but the man that controls the mouth. He can, but only with God's help.

Many of us have been in a situation where we have made a statement, and rather than lose face, we have compounded the problem by continuing to support the statement against our better judgement. For example, we may in a fit of rage declare our annoyance with our boss at work. Whenever he approaches us we treat him with anger and hostility, not because we feel that way towards him, but because we are supporting our earlier statement. Rather than lose face with our colleagues, we act falsely to support the tongue. The uncontrolled tongue is a master of such evil.

We should note too, that not only is there a potential to speak evil, but there is potential to cause great distress, even death. This is seen from the graphic illustration that James uses. It is certain that he did not use the illustration of a forest fire without understanding the impact of what he was writing. The forest fire is one of the greatest threats to cities and towns in many parts of the world. It takes only two things to cause great devastation. A small spark and some dry wood. A flame and fuel are a deadly combination.

Unsanctified speech not only ignites the flame, but also feeds flames already lit. Such speech causes immeasurable damage.

In the context of Christianity, most of us have seen evidence of the spark of an ill-timed or ill-judged word combined with a willingness to gossip. We have also seen the tremendous hurt, pain, distress, and spiritual death that accompany it. Churches have been divided, believers have left the Faith, and potential converts lost to the Kingdom because of uncontrolled tongues.

I am no expert, but it seems from news coverage that firemen seem to have some of their greatest problems trying to extinguish forest fires. In some cases they burn themselves out, in others firemen attempt to contain them or control the direction they take. If they can be contained or stopped from spreading, the danger is almost over.

The comparisons are obvious. Hurtful words, untrue accusations or unholy conversations are not easily extinguished without hurt. Often containment is the only option. What has been said cannot be unsaid, even if apologies are made. The evil nature of some comments result in it being difficult to get to the cause, hence at times we have to contain it and force it back on itself. We are used to seeing the news coverage of great forests ablaze, and the fire services soaking the trees in the path of the fire in order to stop them from igniting. The Christian must seek to recognize the danger of an uncontrolled tongue, and seek to protect himself and those around him from its effect. If we cannot extinguish the evil flame we must protect those in its path.

Evil conversation corrupts the whole body. It destroys everything in its path. Forest fires do not burn around, they burn through. Some years ago I met a man who claimed to have worked in the forests of Canada. He told me how trackers could judge the distance of a forest fire by placing their hands in the nearest river and gauging the temperature of the water. The nearer the fire the warmer the normally ice-cold water became. I was never sure if he was telling the truth, but the principle is certainly true in the spiritual realm!

If you have ever had the misfortune to worship in a church where a tongue was unruly, you will know that the rivers of living water that flow out of a man become affected by the blaze that rages. The water is no longer cool and refreshing but tepid and distasteful. In Revelation 3:16 Jesus found the lives of the

Laodicean believers so lukewarm and unpleasant to the taste that He threatened to spit them out of His mouth.

We should notice too that fire travels and it travels quickly. Yet it is not as fast nor as deadly as words spoken with evil intent. Words are unique, for the further they travel the greater can be their momentum. The more distorted they become the greater is their potential for evil. We should regularly examine our conversation and listen to the conversations of which we are often a part. We should also take into account that we are judging by God's standards not ours.

Do we spark forest fires? Do we fuel other people's fires? If Words of Wisdom and Knowledge are Gifts of the Holy Spirit, where do words of discord, disharmony and discouragement find their origin? Certainly not in God, and surely they ought not to come from His people.

Speech not only has the power for evil; it has great power to bless. Like many things in nature there is a negative and positive side. So too with speech. The same tongue that has the potential to spread evil has the potential to bless.

James is not advocating vows of silence, quite the contrary. Speech is a gift from God. Man before the Fall had the power of speech and in Revelation we read that in heaven we will have the power of speech. What we have is not a command to be silent but a responsibility to use the gift of speech wisely, to bless and not curse.

Throughout James we are challenged to positive action, and this subject is no different. Our speech should be appropriate, holy, sanctified, a positive evidence of what exists within. To the man living without God the tongue is a cause of boasting, but to the man living with God it should be the cause of blessing.

As with the power to do evil, James uses an illustration to make his point clear. The rudder of a boat is one of the smallest parts of the boat, yet it can navigate a boat through the roughest of storms. It is a guiding influence. Irrespective of the size of the boat or the severity of the winds it guides the boat to its destination. It may be small but its role is highly important. Whether it guides for good or evil is dependent not on the rudder, but on the pilot.

This is also true of our speech. The decision to say no to temptation may not be made in the mouth, but it is with the mouth that the answer is given. Speech must be harnessed to our armoury to do good, not to do evil.

It is with our speech that we make a stand for God and His righteousness. It is with our mouths that we make confession of our faith. It is with our lips that we praise God and testify to others. These are examples of the tongue as a rudder in the sense of blessing. They can lead us into calm and blessed waters, and on to our destiny.

Many temptations and potential difficulties can be avoided in the workplace if we make it clear as to where we stand on Christian issues. If we explain our faith, people may draw their own conclusions as to our stability of mind, but it may well avoid unholy and unhealthy conversations in the future. Many of the issues we become entangled with that are unedifying, arise because we have not said where we stand in relation to God.

There is also a second aspect to our speech in regard to our daily life. Not only is our confession before men important, so also is the nature of our conversation. In the world in which we live, the conversation of the believer is as noticeable as light in darkness. The choice of words, use of phrases and tone of voice should reflect a likeness to Christ. Such conversation brings both light and blessing to every situation.

We should consider a more obvious way in which the tongue can be a blessing. It has the ability to bless on God's behalf. Compared to other parts the tongue may only be a small part, but few parts can claim to be God's chosen method of blessing others.

From the earliest of Bible times we see that man is given the power to bless others. This can be achieved by helping and giving, but also by speaking. We have seen how actions speak louder than words in the context of understanding a person's motivation and experience, yet in terms of touching a person's life, we should never underestimate the power of speech.

In John 20 we have a marvellous account of the appearance of the resurrected Jesus to Mary Magdalene. Initially she did not recognize either His voice or appearance, but when He spoke her name she knew in an instant it was Jesus. Such accounts are the dream of preachers, rich in imagery and meaning, presenting endless opportunities. Yet doubtless the plain truth is that the power and authority with which He called her name touched her life.

It was through speech that Jesus proclaimed the message He had been given by God. It was through speech that He proclaimed release to the captives, and it was through speech that He spoke encouragement and hope to the poor and oppressed. The message He brought was delivered by His lips as well as His life.

In my own life there have been many instances where God has blessed me personally through other people. As I recall such times I have to acknowledge that more often than not it was through their speech. I am sure we have all been blessed by inspired and anointed preaching. Likewise we can all recall those people whose prayers, however basic in language and grammar, have touched our hearts and our lives with the sincerity and the genuineness of their faith. Others have caused us to sense the presence of God among us, with songs that have thrilled our spirits and ushered us into the very presence of God. Others have given prophetic utterances, words of encouragement and exhortation that countless times have drawn us closer to the Saviour. I am certain that every Christian could give illustrations of each and add new examples, but the point is clear. What great power the tongue has to bless! We must use the one we have to fan into flame the desire within our brothers and sisters in Christ to serve God with a great passion and commitment.

Every Christian should reflect on how often (or rarely) they offer God the opportunity to bless others, through their speech. Perhaps we should consider this point from a different standpoint. How often do we offer others the opportunity to be blessed by God? Speech is God's most obvious channel and method of ministry. Consider the Spiritual Gifts that are given by the Holy Spirit. The Gifts of Tongues and Interpretation are obviously used via the use of speech, as of course is Prophecy. Consider too, Words of Wisdom and Knowledge usually require the ability to communicate as well as receive revelation.

When do such Gifts become effective? Certainly not before someone uses their voice in a manner of blessing. In Genesis 12:2 we read of God's commitment to Abraham. It was not just a commitment to bless him, but to make him a blessing to others.

Do we bring blessing to those around us? When others need to receive something from God do they look to us? If the answer is no we should consider the way we live and speak.

We should remember that the voice was not given speech for the sake of speech, but for blessing. We must seek God's help and wait upon Him for words that change lives, that lift up the downcast, comfort the lonely, bring hope to the oppressed and joy to the dispirited.

We saw earlier the damage that can be caused by the uncontrolled tongue, but even the devastation it can cause cannot compare with the greatness of a 'word in season'. A calming and peaceable thought to a person in some difficult circumstances can be as refreshing as ice-cool water to a thirsty man on a hot day. What balm there is in anointed speech!

We can heal with our speech, prevent others being hurt, destroy the strongholds of evil, build bridges of reconciliation, all with one timely comment. The sanctified speech of a believer can accomplish the impossible.

We should not let a single day pass when God has not blessed someone through our voice; praying each day for God to use our vocal cords and our tongue, for His glory. If we desire blessing we should use our voices to be a blessing to others.

James also shows that speech is a window to the soul. We have seen that though the tongue is only a small member of the body, and though it has little part in the making of decisions, it expresses the desire of the whole body. It is the reflection of the most inward part of a man.

The way we speak, the words we use, the inference and innuendo we may make, can sometimes say more about us than the subject we use the words to discuss. Food manufacturers often claim that we are what we eat. If we eat healthy food we will be healthy. The Bible tells us we are what we say, for what we say comes out of the heart before it leaves the lips. What we are in our heart is what we are! This makes what we say highly significant.

Jesus also took the subject of speech very seriously. So much so that He taught about it and warned of potential dangers. In Matthew 12:34 He addresses the religious leaders of the day. These were men of whom He was critical, not only because He knew their hearts, but also because He had heard the manner of their conversation. His words represent a serious reprimand, 'You brood of vipers, how can you who are evil say anything good? For out of the overflow of the heart the mouth speaks.'

Some may say that James is contradicting himself. We have seen that it is not what a man says but what he does that is the ultimate proof of his sincerity. That does not make what we say unimportant. Quite to the contrary. What we say is very important, not least because of the words of Jesus.

The seeming contradiction is important for its explanation leads to a deeper understanding. Speech shows what is in the heart. That is clear. Jesus said it, we believe it! How do we know if what is said is true? We check it against the actions. Actions verify what is said. They are the acid test of what we claim. A man may claim to be selfless, but be ungenerous in his giving; because the actions do not prove the words, the heart is revealed as dishonest and deceitful.

James is talking here, not of speech in the sense of confession of faith, but as a fruit of a sanctified heart. In James 1:26 we see that lack of control over speech reflects on the value of our worship, making it worthless. There must not only be harmony between a man's speech and his actions, but there must be consistency in his speech itself. James highlights as examples those who pronounce blessing and at other times curse. Such inconsistency does not come from a heart or life heavily affected by God.

Self-control is itself a fruit of the Holy Spirit living in and guiding us in our daily walk. Control over our speech and language is one of the more obvious signs of His presence within our lives.

The examples given by James show that the tongue has great potential for evil, but James does not stop there. It has the potential for death. For James the picture is one that we have previously discussed. Springs only bring forth water in keeping with the source. A well of salt water that springs up out of the ground will only ever give out salt water. Such is the simplicity of the laws of nature and such is the simplicity of the principles that govern spiritual growth. What we say reflects the source of what is said.

A number of years ago I picked up what I thought was an injury in a training session. A pain appeared in my arm and gradually got worse to the point where I needed treatment. I consulted a physiotherapist who recognized the symptoms immediately. It wasn't a strain or a tear, but a cut that had become infected. With antibiotics it cleared up very quickly.

Sometimes we wonder why God isn't blessing our lives. We assume ourselves to be injured. We think that things beyond our control have conspired to put us on the sidelines. We question this theology and that doctrine, when the problem isn't injury but infection. Listening to our conversation would reveal if there is poison in the system. Poison that kills if it is not addressed with spiritual treatment. Anger, malice, jealousy, rage, disappointment, disillusionment and impatience are just a few examples of poisons that build up within but make themselves known through the tongue. If the poison of evil is to be found within, then the tongue will be restless until it exposes the intent of the heart.

James contrasts the perfect man with the man who cannot control his tongue. The latter is imperfect or incomplete. Perfection must be our aim, but it cannot be found in a life where evil is present and allowed to go on without being addressed.

The life touched by God is a life that is seen and heard to be sanctified. This is important to understand, for the sanctified man is not just different to the world. There are Christians who are different to the world but not sanctified. He is a man who is set apart. Our speech should be dedicated to that which is right, which encourages, builds up and blesses. If that is our manner of conversation, then our lives will be whole, holy, healthy and on the road to perfection.

CHAPTER NINE

Walking in Wisdom

Who is wise and understanding among you? Let him show it by his good life, by deeds done in the humility that comes from wisdom (James 3:13).

James now picks up the subject of leadership once again. Having made it clear that the leader must be in control of his speech he goes one step further on in the process of sanctified living. As we looked at sanctified speech, we looked at the potential for good and evil, but we noted it was decided by intentions. Now we are dealing not with intentions but understanding. The intention to speak for good or bad aside, what we say may also depend greatly upon the level of wisdom, and more importantly, the type of wisdom we possess.

Although wisdom is a word with which we may all be familiar, it is not a word that is easy to define. Its basic meaning is 'skill' or 'cunning', but its more contemporary use conjures up the idea of 'know-how'. In modern life the wise man is the man with the answers, a man who knows what to do in any and every given set of circumstances. This is not too different from the Bible's use of the word. The wise man exercises sound judgement and is a master of appropriateness, knowing what God expects and desires at all times, but more importantly, he is a man that does it.

In James 1:5 we are introduced to true wisdom and told of its origin, God Himself. Here James goes further still in illustrating two points that are fundamental in understanding the whole of this epistle.

Firstly James is dealing with the importance of actions. If we consider that in 1 Corinthians 1:22 Paul writes concerning the desire of the Greeks for wisdom, no doubt based upon his experiences in the city of Athens (Acts 17), we will understand that many failed to link actions and wisdom together. Wisdom was seen as something separate from, if not above, the ordinary day to day affairs of life. It was theoretical and mystical in its nature, not real in the sense of the tangibility of life.

James seeks to strongly challenge this first century view. Christianity is not a topic for debate or discussion only. It was and still is something to be lived and experienced. We can tell a wise man, not because of his answers, but because of his actions.

Secondly there is the ongoing conflict between the natural or earthly and the spiritual or heavenly. This is seen in many ways, but is here illustrated by the difference in the two types of understanding upon which all men build their lives.

There is a popular misconception that spiritual wisdom and earthly wisdom are the same, with the former being sanctified or given God's approval. It is held that the wise man who is converted is still wise, but God works on his wisdom to make it spiritual. As a result of such thinking we try to incorporate into positions of influence within our congregation, those who have demonstrated themselves to be successful through earthly wisdom. Such efforts lead to disaster. In 1 Corinthians 3:19 Paul writes, '. . . the wisdom of this world is foolishness in God's sight . . .' It is not a case of earthly wisdom being different to spiritual wisdom, it is more a case of it being totally opposed. Hence the strong words Paul writes to the Corinthian believers.

The world in its wisdom will claim that the Christian is foolish, but it is their own profession of wisdom that pronounces them foolish. It is not so much the statement they make, but the basis on which the statement is made that is the issue.

Earthly wisdom is based upon self. It advocates self-benefit, self-belief, self-advancement and self-praise. Lives that appear to be good and upright can still be motivated by a flawed wisdom, an earthly wisdom. Some live morally good and respectable, if not admirable lives, but live according to their conscience. This is still based upon what they interpret as acceptable, and coincidence with righteousness is exactly that, coincidence.

This standard by which they live is still one they set for themselves rather than God's. Such wisdom is subtle and manipulative, but that is what we should expect of sin. For sin is at the very foundation of earthly wisdom. It is the putting of your own demands, wishes, choices and decisions before the will of God. If we look at the subject of sin we must look at the events that took place in the Garden of Eden. In Genesis 3:7 we read that the first thing that happened when Adam and Eve disobeyed God was that they became aware that they were naked. Suddenly they became aware of themselves. We often stress that they hid from God, but that was not their initial reaction. They had to deal with their nakedness. Up to that point their eyes were not on themselves, but on God.

People who choose to live by earthly wisdom will notice their own needs before those of others, or the desire of God for their lives. The man who is looking at his own condition before the demands of God on his life is following an earthly not a spiritual wisdom.

One of the greatest weapons in the armoury of the enemy of our souls is our willingness to believe that we personally are the most important person in the world, and that the whole world revolves around us. If we adopt that attitude we will have little care for the consequences of our actions on others.

We criticize profusely the tyrants who, on the world stage dictate to nations and destroy the lives of millions of people in pursuit of their goal of glory and domination. Yet we are often guilty of admiring identical qualities in people who do similar things, but on a smaller scale.

The man who puts his ambition in business, sport or politics before his family but reaches his goal, is looked upon as a success, and possibly hailed as a role model. Yet the price others may have had to pay for his ambition, success, glory and position is basically a result of the same cause as the cost paid by others under a dictator that is openly deplored. The ambition and therefore its effect are different only in regard to scale. Yet sin does not recognize scale. It knows only self raised against the desire of God.

The Christian who plans his life based upon ambition is living by the world's standards and wisdom. Some set themselves targets of achievement or advancement. For example, it may be a certain level of management by a certain age, or a certain size of house or car by a certain time. This is not responsible living, but irresponsible living, because it is based upon personal desire, not a desire to fulfil the destiny planned for us by God.

Such attitudes are not new. Jesus was well aware of them and illustrated such a life with a parable. In Luke 12:13-21 we have portrayed before us a man who is and has everything that earthly wisdom admires and advocates. He is known as the 'Rich Fool'. He was a hardworking farmer who saw that his crops would be bountiful. Being far-sighted he realized the need to pull down his barns and build bigger ones, to store the harvest, as his current ones were not sufficiently large to house the crop. He was obviously hardworking, for good crops, even in good soil with good weather do not grow on their own. Someone has to plant them and tend them. Also he was prepared to invest in and plan for bigger barns. This man was industrious, forward thinking, skilled in agriculture and successful, yet he was described as a fool!

Earthly wisdom builds its barns to store the results of a man's hands, but spiritual wisdom builds them to house God's blessing. Everything this man had done was based on himself. Notice throughout the Saviour's account the use of the personal pronoun 'I' by the man, yet our aim should not be to build storehouses to hold our glory, but God's.

Self-built standards of conduct and belief are one of the greatest obstacles to the Gospel that the Church faces in the intellectual circles of society today. Yet anything based upon a man's own effort is doomed to fail. This is an important area that is deeply affected by New Age teaching and influence. We are told that we as individuals can take to ourselves or develop within ourselves our own deity. It replaces God with self in just the same way that earthly wisdom does. In Genesis 11 we see the account of the Tower of Babel. Expositors and interpreters of the Bible may differ in the detail of their interpretation of the account, but most if not all would agree that man was setting himself up as supreme. It was a project of self-glorification. Hence the harsh lesson God had to teach man.

Earthly wisdom does not know boundaries in its efforts to influence and affect. James deals with the issue of the exploitation by the rich, even to the point of legal action being taken. Why would such a thing happen? For personal gain or advancement! In Acts 16:19 we see this shamefully illustrated. A riot breaks out when the owners of a slave girl who is delivered from an evil spirit, complain. Notice how they were not pleased for her, or grateful that she was free of her torment, anguish and pain. They were more concerned that they had lost their source of income. Earthly wisdom and self-preservation make ungrateful colleagues.

The qualities that are the fruit of earthly wisdom are also deceptive. They may appear to be noble, but often are not. There are those who do what is admired, for the sake of admiration, others for self-esteem, others to prove their virtues to those around them, and some because it fits their view of appropriateness and goodness.

To live such a life is to deny the truth. Truth is the exact representation of things as they really are. Therefore to deny the truth is to misrepresent things and portray them in a manner different to how they really are. Earthly wisdom does exactly that. It misrepresents truth. It is a contradiction of the way that God desires us to live. The way we should live is based upon God not upon self.

There is also a further danger, that of boasting. To boast about our own abilities, success or wisdom is to deny the One who should be living and at work in our lives. It is not wisdom but foolishness that boasts. Remember the danger of an uncontrolled tongue?

If self is at the heart, there is an inevitability that boasting will be at the mouth. If self is at the heart, if it is our guiding principle, we will want others to know of our efforts, abilities, cleverness and accomplishments. If God's place in your life is taken by self, then the worship that is rightly His will be replaced by boasting that is yours.

We must also realize that disorder and evil practices are further fruit of earthly wisdom. We have another example of fruit bearing. In Matthew 11:19 Jesus says '. . . Wisdom is proved right by her actions.' What are actions? Fruit of the tree. The evil tree can only bear evil fruit. Earthly wisdom can produce fruit that *looks* like good fruit, but it cannot produce good fruit.

The word that James uses for 'evil' is a word that has a particular slant on its meaning. It speaks of being of no value or worthless. There is emptiness in earthly wisdom that cannot bear comparison with the blessing of spiritual wisdom. Spiritual wisdom blesses, enlarges and increases the abundance of life. Earthly wisdom empties, it cannot fill, it cannot produce abundant life, for nothing outside of God can bring life at all.

If there is to be found evil or ungodly practice, earthly wisdom will be at the root. Yet there is another fruit of this enemy of

God. That fruit is discord or disorder. We can see the evidence of this within the life of the individual and within the life of a community of people. For the individual, disorder within his life can be a serious problem. It affects every 'good' part of his life. We may have most areas of our life in subjection to God and His standards, but as soon as disorder arrives, every area of our lives becomes subject to difficulty. Temptation will create havoc, for disorder will cause our priorities to lose their significance or importance. We cannot live by two types of wisdom. Attempting to do so will result in instability.

As for the group of believers who experience disorder, equally difficult times lie in store. Selfish ambition and self-interest prove infertile soil for the seed of God's Word and a hostile environment for His Holy Spirit. There is little that is guaranteed to destroy fellowship and sour relationship faster than wisdom that builds its foundation on self. Self is not a team player. The Church of Jesus Christ is not built upon a rock that is broken into fragments, but is itself a collection of fragments that are built together to form one body.

At the beginning of Genesis we read the account of the handiwork of a creative God. If we read the account carefully we cannot help but notice that one of the hallmarks of Creation was order. The laws of nature and of physics are examples of the order that exists, because God is a God of order. Neither trials nor difficulties frighten the believer because they do not disrupt the order within. As that order comes from God nothing that man does can threaten it, unless we choose to allow it. Where chaos and disorder rule, earthly wisdom and sin are never very far away.

We have already seen that spiritual wisdom is very different to earthly wisdom. Because it originates in God it is based upon Him and upon His values, and is therefore different to earthly wisdom from beginning to end. As we have noted, we can learn much about wisdom from its fruit, and spiritual wisdom produces eternal fruit, for it finds its origin in an eternal source, God Himself.

The origin of an idea or motive is akin to wisdom, in that it defines its own nature. One of the potentially most far-reaching fields of science must surely be the study of genetics. It is a subject that deals with heredity and its effects. Characteristics and traits, whether physical or emotional may be a part of our make up, because they existed in our parents or our grand-parents, or even further back in our ancestry. Genetics goes much further than my simple definition, but it also bears witness to the spiritual principle, that whatever is in the tree will come out in the branches. If the source is good, the branches and therefore the fruit will be good.

Now we should be able to see the progression in under-standing. If the origin of spiritual wisdom is different to that of earthly wisdom, the difference will be reflected in their natures. Spiritual wisdom is not based on self or self-motivated but God-based and therefore pure; a point James makes very clearly. He points out that it is 'first of all pure' (James 3:17). This purity is at the core of its nature. This is not about a numerical sequence of the qualities of spiritual wisdom but its primary, overriding and most evident characteristic.

Purity in the spiritual sense is to be seen in the absence of sin, and therefore self. Man's purity was lost in the Garden of Eden because sin imposed itself on what was rightly God's. Wisdom is the same. Spiritual wisdom is pure in that it is untainted by personal desire and preference.

One of the clearest examples of the principle of purity is seen in snow-covered ground. When we describe something as being as pure as the driven snow, what we mean is, it is like snow that is as it has fallen or drifted. It is untouched by human, animal or chemical. Spiritual wisdom is pure in its essence. It is untouched by anything else. It is as God meant it to be. Such wisdom gains nothing from attempts at human enhancement and therefore is void of such vain attempts at improvements.

Spiritual wisdom does not and cannot allow for circumstances, cultural traditions or personal preference to touch upon its purity. It knows the importance and value of the purity of a believer's life. It does not make allowances, for allowances lead to compromise. It will pay more or receive less, rather than succumb to evil. Such purity is not measured in pounds or dollars. It is not seen in material possessions collected. It cannot be measured by man, but it can be seen. It evidences itself not in the quantity but the quality of life.

Purity of life stands tall and burns brightly. Its power is not in its oratory, but in its effect. I remember as a teenager being given a bottle of highly concentrated orange squash. It wasn't a very big bottle, but it seemed to last forever. The reason was the level of concentration of the juice, not the size of the bottle containing it. A watered down or diluted Christianity is not the result of spiritual wisdom, but natural thinking.

During my time at Bible College I was privileged to spend some time with a great man of God. He was a world-renowned Bible teacher with an international ministry, but more importantly a man of great integrity and holiness. One conversation we shared sticks in my memory for it revealed a principle on which we should all attempt to live our lives. He shared how God had revealed to him the importance of personal revelation, for revelation he believed was like water, the nearer the source the purer it would be. I could relate to this principle, for as a boy I used to drink water from mountain springs and streams. The water was always cool and refreshing, especially on a warm summer's day, but the higher up the mountain you went, the purer the water.

As we examine our lives and the events around us that we

can influence we should look to see what level of purity the wisdom we possess brings. The level of purity will reveal the level of spiritual wisdom we possess.

The fruits of spiritual wisdom are further examples of the purity this wisdom possesses. James lists them as 'peace-loving, considerate, submissive, full of mercy and good fruit, impartial and sincere.' Notice how the qualities have a common thread of selflessness, and a likeness to Jesus. Spiritual wisdom does not only find its origin there; it finds its nature there.

If fruit reveals the tree, the qualities that James lists as being indicative of spiritual wisdom leave no doubt as to the nature of spiritual wisdom. What a contrast to earthly wisdom! We are not looking at man-made wisdom as evidenced in the life of the selfish, but heaven-born wisdom as evidenced in the life of Jesus.

We could take the fruit James has listed and look at events in the life of Jesus and notice their presence. To do so would clearly explain why we need to be more like Him. His is the standard we should judge ourselves by. However, it is easier for most of us to measure how far away we are from the worst and console ourselves with mediocrity, than it is to note how far away we are from perfection and Jesus.

Jesus lived His life totally for others. No part was withheld for Himself. Even in the quiet times He shared alone with the Father, His mind was on the need to complete the mission He had been given. The man whose wisdom is spiritual lives the whole of his life for others. The mission he has received from God is of paramount importance. He has no illusions about himself, only a vision of Jesus that goes before him.

For many of us, illusion is something we have to deal with. If we do not have false or deceptive views of ourselves, we are not frightened by the truth about ourselves. The easiest way to avoid being disillusioned is to not have illusions to start with. The spiritual wisdom that all Christians should live by knows no disillusionment, for it is not looking for personal benefit. Disillusionment is for those living and working for themselves. The Christian serving God will not know disillusionment for his hope, ambition, strength and confidence is not in himself, but in God. The only disappointment he may experience is the lack of blessing that others seek or receive.

James illustrates this point by showing how peacemakers will reap their reward. Spiritual wisdom sows spiritually, therefore it reaps spiritually. What a difference there is between reaping disorder and righteousness. If disorder is totally opposed to God and His being, righteousness reflects His very being. It describes Him, and its very existence is a source of blessing.

God is pleased with righteousness. It is the seed we are called to sow and the harvest we are called to reap. It signifies our relationship with God is right from start to finish. In short we are holy.

Fundamental to our life on earth is the realization of the destiny to which God has called us. In order to receive from God we need to sustain a relationship with Him. Earthly wisdom drives us further from God whereas spiritual wisdom draws us closer. The reason for this is the relationship between God and righteousness.

We may pride ourselves on the closeness of our walk with God, but we may also deceive ourselves by the same token. The fact that we know God says more about Him than it does about us. To learn about ourselves we should look at our lives and compare the fruit of those lives with the fruit of spiritual wisdom. It may be that from time to time we should look at events that have taken place and consider how we have acted and reacted in light of the fruit of spiritual wisdom. Our actions are not proven right by comparison with the actions of others involved but by comparison with the fruit of spiritual wisdom. Such a comparison takes away the complacency of being 'better' than others and replaces it with a realization of the perfection of Jesus.

The warning is a serious one. Earthly wisdom detracts and distracts from God. Conversion is not the only time in life when we need to repent. Only spiritual wisdom can draw us closer to God, and to live another way is to need to repent. There is only one direction we want our paths to go, and that is nearer to, not further from the Father. The only way we can walk that road is to walk in spiritual wisdom. Without such wisdom we will not reap a harvest of righteousness, and without such wisdom we will not please God.

CHAPTER TEN

The Matter of Motivation

. . . you ask with wrong motives . . . (James 4:3).

As we have looked at the message James presents to his readers, we cannot have failed to notice the power and authority it possesses. He has not failed in his responsibility of presenting the truth of the Christian message, and the responsibility of Christian living. Personally I am gripped by the importance he places upon the heart of a man being right with God. Here again he deals with that very important issue. The man of God is a man with the right inclinations. His desire is always such and therefore his priorities are always spiritual.

This is the kind of living that lifts a man from mediocre Christian living and puts him on a spiritual level. It is the implementing of such teaching that affects the effect of a believer, not only in his dealings with God, but also in his dealings with the world. Until God, through His Word and Spirit, has an effect upon us we will have no or little effect upon those around us.

We have to understand that here James is digging deep. He is not looking at the surface of a believer's life, but deep inside his heart. While we are often quick to point out that there are no accidents in the way God deals with man, we must accept responsibility for the things we do, and how we react to whatever comes our way. There has to be a realization that what we do and say does not just happen, but is itself a result, not a cause. It is a result of who and what we are. This is another case of like producing like, and the principle of fruit bearing.

Many within society find great difficulty with this issue when they try to deal with problems in their lives. They approach the areas of concern as though they were the cause, when in truth they are the effects. If a tree is infected, you do not treat the fruit, but the tree. In order to sustain life a tree needs water; but it is not to the fruit but to the roots we give the water necessary to sustain life.

It is often quoted that in 1904 at the time of the great revival in Wales, Police stations closed down due to the reduction in crime. This was due to the problems being addressed rather than the symptoms.

The Christian is often no different in terms of dealing with symptoms and not causes. There are often issues we try to address by dealing with the results, rather than asking God to show us why such things are happening. The answer to a leaking roof is not a bucket in the attic, but a repair to the roof.

We must look with seriousness and sincerity at what James instructs with regard to motives and priorities. It is the order of priorities within our lives that will show our motives. If serving God is our greatest motive, rising early to pray, staying up late to read, missing a meal in order to fast and pray or missing out on social events to be at our local church working or worshipping, will be a pleasure not a chore. If our motivation is not focused on God, if the wisdom we live by is not spiritual, then we will either not do those things or we will do them grudgingly. They will gradually slip down our list of priorities.

Wrong motives and wrong priorities will without any shadow of a doubt have an effect upon the believer's life; an effect that can be devastating. Worse still is the fact that such effects are not limited in their effect to the believer alone, but to all he comes in contact with. We have a responsibility to sow our lives into the Kingdom of God, an exercise that affects others. Such is our calling. We are not isolated individuals, but a community of people who are being built together into the Kingdom of God. If we look at the illustration in the New Testament of the Church being a building, we will realize that we must be more than just bricks. We must be joined together. Loose bricks will cause a building to either become derelict or simply crumble. Seen any churches like that recently?

Apart from my student days, the whole of my life has been spent in the valleys of south Wales, a place with an abundance of closed churches. In the vast majority of cases they did not close because of faulty buildings. They closed because the people who used to gather inside were either no longer joined together or no longer alive. In either case the effect is the same. When motives are moved away from God other people are very quickly affected.

How does one snowflake become an avalanche? By joining with and therefore affecting other snowflakes. Christians can, through unrighteous motives, affect others adversely until what is not a problem, becomes a problem. In much the same way, for very different reasons, the opposite happens when Christians have a right and holy attitude to each other. When this happens, events do not snowball out of control but avalanche under God's control.

The individual Christian has a responsibility before God to guard the gift He has placed within him. The easiest, most far-reaching and vital method is to ensure that the priorities we place upon our time, talents, finances, plans and hopes reflect not on what the natural man desires, but what God desires for us.

We have already been made aware that the fields around us are white as in harvest. The problem the Kingdom of God faces is lack of labourers to go forward and reap the harvest. These may be often repeated truths, yet many of us have difficulty grasping them. A harvest doesn't stick around waiting for the farmer to decide what priority it has in his life. If he doesn't reap the crop when the crop is ready then he will lose it. Lost to many of us in the teaching of Jesus is that a harvest is being lost! We should also ask how so many people could claim to be labourers and yet so little harvesting is taking place? The answer is found in Matthew 25 and the illustration that Jesus used of sheep and goats. He makes it clear that a labourer is not one who claims to be a labourer, but one who actually labours. They are those, whose priorities are based upon the needs of others, not desires for self-benefit, or self-advancement.

If it is the case that you feel the call to the service of our King, and desire to be a labourer, you need to start by examining your priorities. There is no room for doubt or a double-mind. Such attitudes, as we have seen, lead to instability. Serving God and living for Him must be our first and greatest priority.

To be a labourer but not desire service above all else, including personal gain and advancement, is to fail before we start. Modern-day Christianity finds monasticism and the lifestyle of monks a thing of the past and therefore difficult to understand. Yet, when we consider the sacrifices many of them made, and the reasons they made them, we can start to understand why so many of them such as Martin Luther were so greatly used of God to shape Church history. Unselfish living and spiritual priorities have been the hallmarks of labourers of the Kingdom in every generation, and will continue to be so until Jesus returns. How many God-given gifts and talents have had their potential unfulfilled, simply because of wrong motives and unholy priorities?

James outlines and details for us the cause, characteristics and the cure for unrighteous motivation.

The cause of unrighteous motivation is selfish ambition, the very opposite to righteous motivation. James highlights two aspects by using the words 'kill' and 'covet'. The selfish man is prepared to put personal ambition and possessions before God's standards and will. This man sees others and the things they possess as a threat to his own exaltation and happiness.

We can also see that the selfish man bases his actions on, and is therefore motivated by pleasure. The idea in James 4:3 that such people 'spend' what they have on pleasure is not confined in its meaning to finance. James is conveying the idea that their very lives are 'spent' or consumed in pursuit of fleshly or earthly desires. They are totally consumed by their ungodly desires. The ultimate price we will pay if we pursue sin is ourselves. Our destiny, our peace, our life and our very soul is the price that is paid in pursuit of selfish ambition.

As Christians it is important that we understand the account and implications of the Fall of Man. It is not that we need to make our theology consistent, though that is obviously important, but that we might rightly apply the lessons of Scripture to our daily walk with God. James 4:6 tells us that God stands opposed to the proud. What brought about the Fall? Pride! This is not about the warm feeling that we DIY failures feel when we make something out of a flat pack kit that stands on its own, nor the feeling a father feels when his son scores the winning goal for the school football team. We are talking about that belief within that exalts us and our desires into a place of preference over the will of God.

One of the significant difficulties that Christians have faced in recent generations has been the idea of open sin and hidden sin. We must treat with caution the acceptability of one sin against another. Open sins such as adultery have been seen as disqualifying a person from service, while less open sins have often been overlooked. We would not allow murderers to preach from our pulpits, but men full of pride could and probably do preach with regularity, even though pride is an abomination to

God. It doesn't justify murder or adultery, but it does reflect the inconsistency with which we treat sin. Of course God forgives sin, including pride, but repentance must be evident before forgiveness and blessing flows.

We must guard against those who claim to be building the Kingdom of God, or labouring in the Master's harvest, yet are really building their own empire and labouring to satisfy their own ego. Matthew 7:15-23 makes it clear that such people will exist, but it also describes their destiny, and it is not a harvest of righteousness.

Every believer sees things that are material, or goals and ambitions in others that they admire. This is not sin, nor is it pride. As a teenager I always admired athletes who could run a sub-four minute mile. In fact I still do, probably more now than then! The only difference between now and twenty-five years ago is that now I don't even bother to dream about doing it myself. To admire such an achievement, to want to understand what it takes or how it is achieved is not sin. To dedicate my time and effort to achieve it when it is not God's destiny for my life is sin. Furthermore it is pride, because it is the elevation of self above the will of God.

As a result of seeing this point we can now go on further and recognize that pride, as the cause of ungodly motivation, like its father the devil is subtle. For pride can manifest itself in the form of something that is wholesome and good. If a young man leaves Christian ideals behind and lives by what is outwardly seen and judged to be the world's standards, we all, whether publicly or privately, deplore his actions. Yet if the same young man ignores the gift that God has placed within him for ministry and chases the wealth and glamour of commerce and business, many would sing his praises for the single-minded way he worked and provided for his family. If he tithes his probably large salary he'll be even more highly exalted within his church.

Yet all the time he is being driven by pride, exalting its own selfish ambition above the will of God.

Any and every Christian with a desire to serve God has to become increasingly aware that sin has to be dealt with, not by legalistic measures, but the power of God's Spirit dwelling within us. Legalistic living will tell us which words we should omit from our vocabulary, the people we should avoid contact with, the practices we should forsake and the places we should not frequent. None of these things will deal with the issue of motivation.

Legalism will deal with the symptom, but not the cause. Yet for all that, many would prefer legalism to waking up to the fact that they are responsible for their own motivation, whether righteous or unrighteous. It is on such motivation that God views and judges our actions.

I have said that the believer should become 'increasingly aware' of the need to deal with sin. The phrase is carefully chosen. As we draw closer to God in our relationship, the effect of sin becomes more noticeable. The closer to God we grow, the purer our lives need to become. The 'Shadow of the Almighty' that Psalm 91 tells of is a holy place, a place set apart from the world and its standards.

The very first thing we see in James 4 with regard to the characteristics of ungodly motivation is the evidence of conflict. In the context of which James is writing, conflict shows a certain evidence that God is not present and active. It is worthy of note that one of the first comments God had to make after the Fall was to announce the presence of conflict. In Genesis 3:15 we see enmity between mankind and the serpent. This conflict, through sin, is reflected in lives that are governed by sin.

We see from James 4:1 that there is the presence of conflict within the life of a believer when that life is not wholly given over to God. The spirit within the Christian is disturbed and distressed by the very presence of earthly desires, and is even more greatly aggrieved by submission to such desires.

When such a picture exists we find ourselves living outside the divine plan for our lives. Suddenly nothing fits the great jigsaw that makes up our lives. To see the pattern and to see where the pieces fit, we must see the picture as God sees it.

We have to recognize an important distinction here. Is this battle within our lives, cause or effect? Or could it even be both?

James makes it clear that this battle that wars within is in fact the effect of wrong or misplaced priorities, which is producing fruit after its kind, i.e. bad fruit. The fruit of selfish desire is more than bad fruit in the sense of being 'distasteful'; it is a fruit that adversely affects all other fruit with which it comes into contact. Selfish motivation is among the most virulent forms of spiritual disease known to man.

As James writes of these desires that cause a battle within the believer, the inference and the truth go much deeper than what may appear on the surface. This is no minor conflict or military skirmish, but outright war. A battle may involve no more than two groups in conflict, but war involves strategy and planning as well as the presence of battles.

So it is with selfish desires and priorities. They not only affect the way we act now but they also create the problems we will face tomorrow, for they affect our hopes and ambitions.

When I speak to teenagers especially, I feel compelled to challenge them on the subject of planning their lives. Financial and relationship commitments must be made on the basis of God's plan for their lives, not on how they see the future or how their parents see their future. Many make wrong long-term commitments and suffer as a result. Impetuosity and poor advice are often co-conspirators with ungodly motivation. In Hebrews 12 we are encouraged to leave aside or behind us the things that would slow us down in our service to God. If our priorities are wrong we will slow down until we stop.

We have noticed the far-reaching effects of selfish priorities, but we should also be aware of how deeply they affect us. This is the avalanche effect in operation. Sin is self-perpetuating. It grows and multiplies in both frequency and intensity.

One significant effect of this type of living is unanswered prayer. This is a raw nerve for many of us. While it is wrong to surmise that all unanswered prayer is due to the presence of sin in our lives, if our motivation is earthly how will we recognize answered prayer when prayer is a spiritual exercise? There are times when God answers prayer but we do not receive blessing because we do not see it, or we are looking in the wrong place or not looking at all.

If we do not receive because we do not ask, we should be able to recognize the problem we have. If the answer is not forthcoming because of wrong motives, we will become pragmatic in our interpretation of events. We will interpret the unanswered prayer as being an answer in itself and assume God's plan is different to our request and change the request we make; whatever the consequence in loss of blessing. When we are motivated spiritually we persist because the spirit within us witnesses with God's Spirit that we are right to persist and wait. Though it tarries we wait for it. Faith, as we have seen previously, does not give in, but grows and yearns with expectancy.

Prayers driven by personal desire for gain or advancement when unanswered leave bitterness within our spirit. The reason is found in the nature of the fruit that personal and selfish priorities produce. When our hope is for others, we do not take disappointment personally. When motives are insincere and the reason is for gain we take all things personally.

Selfish desires, especially if they lead to unanswered prayer result in emptiness. James 4:2 tells us that we miss out. We do not possess what we could and sometimes what we should have, because we ask with the wrong motivation. Commentators may discuss the nature of what James' readers did not possess, but the truth is they possessed little that was of real worth to them. To use a modern phrase, they were empty vessels. They may make the most noise, but they experience little satisfaction. Only lives filled by God are blessed.

We see too, that the bad fruit produced by personal conflict produces further bad fruit. This is the nature of sin. Unfulfilled personal desire will produce a chain reaction of envy and jealousy, followed closely by quarrelling and fighting. Again we return to conflict, but this time it is not conflict within the believer, but conflict among believers.

Selfish motivation will inevitably bring conflict within the believer's life and bring conflict with others. It is inevitable because of its very nature. It wants, above all things, what it considers the very best for itself, and will therefore be in conflict with others who desire what is righteous and good. It will also be in conflict with those who are like-minded. Two selfish people do not make for a harmonious relationship.

Remembering the context of this discussion we should ponder such thoughts in the context of church life. Suddenly James has illuminated brightly the very reason for so much church strife and disorder. Before we know blessing in our churches, we need to know unity. Yet before unity, comes something very important. Many seem to think that it is uniformity, but it is not. It is singleness in the integrity of our motivation. God doesn't withhold blessing because we fail; He knows our imperfections and loves us all the same, but He does desire and expect that we be united by a single desire to do His will, whatever the cost.

Envy and jealousy are not fruits of righteousness and

therefore do not lead to reconciliation and peace, but deceit and therefore death. The Parable of the Sower (Matthew 13) is very enlightening and teaches us many lessons. One that is often overlooked is the lesson of the soil. We can affect the quality of the soil by the way we live our lives. Through kindness and patience we can prepare an appropriate resting-place for the seed. Through bitterness, envy, jealousy, deceit and ungodly motives we can prevent the seed from having a good chance of germinating and taking root. How many have come into our services and left before the seed could take root, because they have seen the conflict of selfish motives? If this is not bad enough we then blame God for not giving us increase of harvest.

James also stresses again the danger of friendship with the world. Here he pinpoints a dilemma that has plagued believers of all ages and every generation. It is a dilemma of under-standing. A dilemma of understanding a difference. That difference is the difference between being a 'friend of sinners' as was Jesus, and a 'friend of the world'. To be the former is to bring life to the lost while to be the latter is to live outside the plan and purpose of God for our lives, and to never fulfil the destiny that is rightly ours in God.

The difference exists not in some theological wordplay, but in the reality of Christian living. To be a friend of a sinner is not to endorse worldly or earthly wisdom and all that it stands for, but to recognize the worth of a person in the eyes of God. Every person on earth needs to be shown love. To do so is to reflect the life of Jesus that should be within us. Friendship with the world is not about befriending the lost or the lonely, it is rather about embracing and being a part of a set of values and ideals that are totally opposed to the destiny of the believer.

I have met many who, having been confused by the difference have found themselves struggling spiritually. They have mistakenly considered what was friendship with the world to be friendship with the lost and needy.

Personal experience in the world of sport has taught me the importance of knowing your own motives. I have met Christians whose number one priority in sport was to win others for Jesus. They became the friend of sinners, but not friends with the world. Fame, success, popularity and personal reward were so far down their list of priorities that they were out of sight, if they existed at all. For others this was not the case. Living under Grace is not licence to become a free agent, but a responsibility to live for God.

I have never felt comfortable with the view that if God helps us win or succeed in material matters the world will admire and be won to God. This sits very uneasily with the belief that the blood of the martyrs was the seed of the Church.

It has been my own personal conviction that people are touched not so much by seeing lives that are without problems, but by seeing how the power of God makes a difference in overcoming problems. This is not achieved by taking the world's standards of selfish living, or ignoring God's standards, but by embracing all that God desires of us and for us. We have to be honest with ourselves and with God, and consider our motives and involvement with the world in which we are called to live.

There is another evidence of ungodly motivation that we should consider, and this is found in James 4:11. It is an issue that we have more than touched on in passing in previous chapters; the subject of the tongue. We have already seen the damage that an unruly tongue can cause. Here we see the same danger in the context of a proud and selfish person. If in his heart such a man should exalt his own desires above those of God, is it surprising that his tongue will make pronouncements that only God can make? Slander and judgement go hand in hand, for it is not ours to judge or slander. Only God can judge and only He can give the authority to judge. We must be very careful of what is in our heart. For what is hidden and out of sight in our heart today may be on our lips and out in the open tomorrow.

We must consider one other effect of unrighteous motivation. This is an effect that is treated by God as adultery. Every person that becomes a Christian enters into a relationship with God. This relationship, like all relationships can only grow if both sides remain faithful. Fidelity is vital. We have God's assurance of faithfulness, but when a Christian lives by the world's standards or flirts with its wisdom, he has not only become unfaithful or adulterous but has shown contempt to God.

True to the Christian message, James does not leave his readers without an answer, nor without hope. Also true to the message, he makes it clear that the answer is to be found in drawing near to God. As we seek to address this important issue in our lives we can be very sure that as we draw closer to God, He will draw closer to us.

In order for this to take place James highlights the steps that need to be taken, and he begins with the key.

Self must give way to submission. The basis of our relationship with God is submission to Him and to His plan. This is not a passive giving up or surrender, but an active decision to become subservient to God. We choose to allow God to exercise His authority over us, and choose to accept it. We do not battle to gain our own way but live and work towards fulfilling the divine purpose for our lives. Before this can happen pride must give way to humility, a quality that God honours and values most highly. To James, humility is more than the means of returning to God; it is the gateway to receiving God's grace.

In Matthew 18:2-4 Jesus having called a small child to stand among His disciples pointed out another of the great spiritual principles of Christian living. The greatest person in God's

Kingdom is so not because of his talent or ability, but because he possesses the humility of a little child.

It is out of such an attitude of heart and way of life that obedience and faith are born. Obedience without humility is not true obedience. It cannot be, for it does not possess the spirit that makes obedience what it is. Some will obey, while others carry out instructions. The latter may find it suits their purpose to do so, though it is not then obedience. True obedience is not and cannot be born in a heart full of pride.

Humility does not seek to belittle or degrade the individual; it simply accepts the exalted position of God as the most important principle in life. Everything that is done, owned and hoped for is tied into this principle. The humble man deems himself to have died with Christ and now only lives to God.

This is a vital part of the renewed relationship with God, and expresses a very different, in fact an opposite, attitude to the one prevailing in the heart of the proud. James is looking for a substantial change of heart and attitude.

We see that rejoicing must give way to repentance, without which there is neither forgiveness nor drawing near to God. There is no basis of trust on which to build a relationship, and this has to be addressed before a man can draw near to God.

As the cause of the problem James has highlighted is sin, repentance must be present in the remedy. All sin, whatever form it takes, must be acknowledged and repented of. It does not go away on its own and it simply cannot be ignored or forgotten.

There must be genuine signs of repentance. Submission to the will of God is vital, but James goes further and calls for grief, mourning and even wailing. Why?

There is no virtue in misery, and joy is an important fruit of the believer's life. James is not challenging an expression but an attitude. Before the joy of a relationship with God can be experienced and expressed, a man must feel sorrow for his sin.

We are quick to criticize emotions and teach that faith comes before feelings, but we should also recognize a man's emotions can also reveal what is in his heart. If we do not feel and act upon repentance, we have not dealt with the issue of sin. It is the response to the work of God's Spirit upon our hearts as well as our minds.

A further evidence of true repentance is seen through a man's actions. Sin must also give way to separation. The significance of the instruction to 'Wash your hands', is not just seen as being symbolic of spiritual cleansing, but should also be seen in the context of disowning. The life in a right relationship with God is a life that practices separation from the world. This is not isolation, but submission to a new master.

James also adds one other key element in dealing with ungodly motivation, in that yielding must give way to resisting. The man who formerly yielded to sin must resist. This is not achieved by some self-purifying rite or self-development ritual, but by resisting sin at its root. We do not resist ourselves, but the evil one. Hence we need more than positive thinking; we want 'God' thinking.

If we resist the devil he will flee from us. He only has the power to achieve his ends if we allow him to. Resistance is guaranteed to foil his efforts. There is a double action here for the repentant man to carry out. Resisting and returning. To resist the devil without returning to God is to attempt to win in our own strength. If we choose that course of action it will not be long before our resistance wanes and a return to sin is inevitable. Return without resistance, however, will also lead to a further breakdown in our relationship with God. Both actions have to be carried out.

If we are living with ungodly motives ruling our lives, we must put all of these steps in place. Some will not be enough. Failure to do so will leave us short of our destiny in God and the standard our God expects of us.

CHAPTER ELEVEN

The Duty of Destiny

. . . What is your life? You are a mist that appears for a little while and then vanishes (James 4:14).

Of the many questions that James must have asked during his life and ministry, few, if any, could have carried with them the impact that this one does. I have sat around the tables of university and college alike, and around the canteen tables of factories with the very same question as the topic of conversation. Surely this question is the biggest question that faces the vast majority of people today.

Driving home one day late in 1998 I turned on the radio in my car and found that I had tuned in part way through a discussion on the attempts of science to prolong human life. Recent developments had raised the possibility that in the not too distant future, people would be able to live to ages in the region of 120 to 150 years old. There was one overriding and continually reappearing concern, the concern that this did nothing to guarantee either the quality or the meaningfulness of life.

In our earnestness to preach to the unconverted we preach that life does not begin until you have met with Jesus, but when they become Christians we sometimes fail to remind them that the new life they receive at conversion does not end there.

If we do not come to terms with the very purpose for our existence, we will not fulfil that purpose in our lives. Before a Christian can live in the blessing of abundant life, he must understand it. Straightening out his theology does not do this, nor attaining saintly levels of holiness; it is done by understanding how that life has come to him.

Destiny is one of the words that God is breathing into His Church in our generation and bears great influence on the subject of the purpose of life. God has an individual destiny for every believer. This is not a simple fate that a sovereign but impersonal god has planned. Such a belief would leave us all disappointed, helpless and hopeless, but the destiny we have in God is glorious. Life without destiny becomes only the passing of time, while life with destiny is to take every precious moment and wring from it every drop of the presence and grace of God.

You and I have been given a destiny, a plan and a purpose chosen for us by God. It has been hand carved by the God of Creation and shaped by the finger that sculptured the commandments at Sinai. It is written by the finger of the Father, and sealed with the blood of the Son. It is ours! It carries our name, and is more personal than a fingerprint or DNA code. Scientists can take a hair and identify a DNA code, but when God sees a hair of your head, He sees a name, a plan, a purpose and a destiny that pre-dates time, that was born in eternity.

In Jeremiah 1:5 we have the record of how God speaks to the young prophet. The call of the young man to service is famous, but notice the way God reassures him of the call. Even before he was conceived in his mother's womb he was known to God, called of God and destined by God to be great. Though Jeremiah's life and ministry may be very different to ours, the God who calls and destines His people is the same.

This God-inspired destiny is ours, as is the choice to accept it or ignore it, to fulfil it or miss out on it.

It is with such a challenge and responsibility in mind that James lays down the question before us. It is not a question for the medical profession, or the psychologists. It is not for the politician or the philosopher. It is for men and women like you and I who have our destiny before us.

To live as God desires us we must focus on the calling He has given to us, a calling that includes our destiny and our very purpose for living. Some will point out that the purpose of our lives is to worship and to serve God, and that this is man's greatest achievement and purpose. This is a powerful and persuasive argument, yet it is not entirely true. The reason it is not entirely true is that it is not all-inclusive of man's purpose of existence.

In Hebrews 11 we see the story of Abraham. God called him to leave his home and to go to a place the whereabouts of which he was not told. To obey was his duty; to reach the place was his destiny. What would have happened if Abraham had worshipped God and served God but stayed where he was? We must not confuse duty with destiny. To serve and worship is our duty, to receive what God has planned for us is our destiny. Serving and worshipping are vital parts of a believer's life, but so is reaching out for our destiny in God.

James has strong advice to give on the subject of destiny, and he begins with a continuation of a well-known theme. Destiny cannot be achieved through personal ambition, desires or planning. It is not the result of what I may want. James makes it clear that such a view is foolish and sinful. This is earthly wisdom and pride at work. James is building on his earlier themes.

This is important to understand for the world applauds ambition. Unfortunately in some circles, so do Christians. We have looked previously at the story of the Rich Fool in Luke 12. He had ambition, but it did not help in realizing his destiny; his life and death stands as a stark but clear warning to the result of ambition outside of God's plan and destiny for our lives.

There is a further danger that we confuse desire with ambition. To desire something is to yearn or long for it, while to have ambition is to aspire to it. To aspire means to reach upwards. Ambition speaks of personal advancement. Yet the man who reaches his destiny will say of Jesus the same as John the Baptist said: 'He must become greater; I must become less' (John 3:30). John had desire, but it was without the accompaniment of ambition. There were no hidden agendas of achievement, simply a ministry to be carried out and a destiny to be fulfilled.

In 1 Timothy 3:1 Paul writes of those who had a desire for a certain position within the Church. He commends the office in question, but what he has to say does not always show clearly in English translations. He is commending those who want to carry out the office, not those who want to wear the title. The ambitious don't want the responsibility, they want the glory. They don't want the work, they want the worship. To desire to work for God is a right quality, to desire the title is not.

Now we see clearly why the Bible shows the need for those who are called to lead to have a servant's heart. There are two things you will not find in the ambitious. The first is a servant's heart and the second is a calloused hand.

The writer of Psalm 84:10 captures this theme beautifully when he writes '. . . I would rather be a doorkeeper in the house of my God than dwell in the tents of the wicked.' Ambition does not worship God for God's sake. In 1 Corinthians 1 Paul explains how God has taken ordinary people and made them into extraordinary people. People who think they are extraordinary will only ever achieve the ordinary, however great their ambitions. An ordinary person, who accepts his destiny in God, forgoes personal ambition and becomes extraordinary.

The Old Testament is filled with illustrations of such people. We should take Moses as an example. The early part of his life saw him trained to be a leader, to be ambitious, to be a prince. This was the way that children in his position were raised. Yet before he could reach his destiny God made a shepherd out of him. Moses went from the position of a prince to an occupation that was so insignificant that it was despised in the eyes of the Egyptians. To the Egyptians, a man thought to be a somebody had become a nobody, but in God's eyes he had become a somebody. What was left by the removal of ambition was filled by a more than worthy replacement in faith.

Moses did not learn self-dependence in the wilderness, but dependence upon God. Ambition cannot recognize faith; it plans it out of its life. It limits God to what is humanly possible. It is not those whose ambition is to have healing ministries that are likely to see the sick healed. It is those who pray for the sick. There is a difference. Too many sit back and wait until they have been told they have a ministry before they carry it out. It seems logical, it seems reasonable, but it's not the way that God works. Those who have ministries such as healing, evangelism or pastoral care don't wait until they get a title or recognition from a committee. They are moved by the need. They are not focused on themselves or on what others think of them, but on God and the need of others. If we see a road accident we phone for help. We don't go home and wait to get a job with a telephone company before we ring for help.

Drivers, whose attention has wandered from the road ahead cause traffic accidents. Whether distracted by something on the pavement or simply admiring the scenery it does not matter. Road safety depends on the driver looking at the road. Spiritually, life is no different. Ambition is a distraction that brings with it many an accident and many a casualty.

Ambition will not wait for doors to open, but rather looks for doors to open. That is not the way that the Christian life and ministry works. The miraculous happens when we do not have to open doors. It is the intervention of a destiny-planning God that sees the miraculous happening in our lives. Destiny originates in the heart of God, not in the ambitions of a man.

We should also be aware that neither ambition nor ability can bring about our destiny. The world in which we live prizes both qualities, and the current younger generation in our nation has grown up in a society that worships the entrepreneurial spirit. The kind of spirit that takes ambition and ability and turns it into success, usually making a fortune on route. Such people would relate very closely to the people James is writing about. The world may be highly impressed but God most certainly is not. This is not because He is mean and doesn't want His people to prosper, but because the destiny of every believer is greater than can be achieved in his own ability.

People have extraordinary abilities in a vast array of ways. Commerce, business, politics, sport and entertainment are all areas where ability can reap rich rewards in the eyes of the world. Yet to the Christian, ability that is not mixed with faith becomes inability. It sounds self-contradictory, but you cannot trust in God and trust in yourself. Notice how in 1 Corinthians 1 Paul writes that few of the Corinthians who were rich in this world's possessions, positions and power had become mighty in God. You cannot trust in nor can you serve two masters. Such lives are double-minded and therefore unstable.

One of the clearest examples of how our strengths can become our weaknesses is seen in the world of finance. Some commentators seem to think that Judas Iscariot looked after the disciples' money because he probably had some kind of financial background. Yet for all this he was a thief and thoroughly dishonest. As unlikely as that may seem to some people, consider the large-scale frauds that we occasionally read about in newspapers. It is not janitors and porters but company directors and accountants that are usually responsible. People with ability and talent appear more likely to attempt to carry out such crimes, not least because they think they are clever enough to carry it off.

We say that knowledge is power, but it is also temptation. Ability plus ambition, minus faith, is a very unhealthy formula.

The best church treasurers are not those with accountancy qualifications, but those with faith. Ask any minister who has undergone building or expansion projects, or has had to present budgets and plans for investing money in church ministries, which of the two he would prefer. The one gives help; the other support. Accountants are expensive to hire, but men of faith are above value.

Irrespective of how much ability we possess, nothing of eternal value can be carried out except by faith. We saw earlier an example from the life of Moses. He had the benefit of what surely had to be the greatest training and upbringing the world at that time had to offer. The Egyptian Court had every advantage there was to be had, but it could not equip him for the destiny to which God had called him. In his time in the desert alone with God he learned that faith accomplishes everything that ability cannot.

Imagine if David had fought Goliath in his own strength. The outcome would have been different. Yet he had already learned the same lesson as Moses. Samson had unequalled strength, not because of his training programme, but because of God's strength. To have ability is not a sin, but to put your trust in it is.

One of the verses in the New Testament that has influenced me greatly is Acts 4:13. It tells us that those who saw Peter and John were amazed at their courage and apparent ability, when they had no formal education. These men were living above anything that their curriculum vitae or school record could have dared to suggest. There was nothing in their background or family history that suggested they would perform miracles and become leaders of men. Yet they had been with Jesus, a fact that shapes destiny more than any other influence.

We have to realize that ability can be limited to how we think and how we act. No amount of debating lessons is going to convince a man that he is a sinner and needs saving. No amount of medical training will speak healing or call forth the dead.

Throughout my ministry I have spent a lot of time speaking to fellow Christians about the Baptism of the Holy Spirit and the supernatural Gifts that accompany it. Some from more formal backgrounds have come to experience this wonderful gift from God and the blessing that accompanies the experience. Others have paid some lip-service, but no more. What has been noticeable, is that some who do not believe in its relevance, put their trust in their own abilities. Yet often something happens; their own ability fails them. When the need is greater than our training, our ability or our understanding, where is our help? Who is our hope?

The answer is a miraculous God who still works miracles in and through His people. There are times when we have to leave what we think is ability behind, because it is a hindrance. Trust in our ability stifles God. It limits Him to the natural.

When you are working with people that the best-trained and equipped experts in society have failed to help, the answer is to look beyond ability and training to a God who indwells and fills His people with His Spirit. We can look to a God who causes us to go beyond our natural ability into the supernatural realm of miracle-working power.

How great then is our destiny? The answer is to be found in the combination of two factors, the greatness of God and the size of our faith.

If we want a human-sized destiny, we should trust in ourselves. If we want a destiny that is mighty, that shakes nations and shapes history, we should look, not at what we can do for ourselves, but at what God can do in us, for us and with us.

In the Sermon on the Mount Jesus talks of the importance of storing up treasure in heaven, treasure which is safe and secure, eternal in its nature and eternal in its reward. Natural ability can only glorify the natural man; hence it only produces natural rewards. God-given abilities are glorifying to God and therefore are eternal.

We must be sure that we do not confuse natural gifts and talents with spiritual gifts. Some believe that gifted orators are the prophets of today. Not everything that we may deem to be gifts from God are actually so. A genetic predisposition or tendency is not the type of gift from God that we are talking of here. There is a sense in which all gifts come from God because He is the giver of all good gifts and the giver of life. Some confuse this with the supernatural Spiritual Gifts that cannot be learned, earned, inherited genetically nor handed down by man. These Gifts heal the sick, raise the dead, cast out demons, feed multitudes and triumph over nature. These are the kind of gifts that God has planned to be a part of our destiny.

We must see too that destiny is not achieved through affluence; yet for many, money figures largely in any conversation on destiny. Many of us spend our lives in pursuit of affluence and encourage our children and grandchildren to do the same. Very few people I know encourage their children to stay in full-time education because they want them to be educated; they do so because they see it as a means to affluence.

There is a thread of logic here, but unfortunately it is the logic of the world. Of course it is not difficult to understand how those who raised their children in relative hardship want their children to have easier lives than they did. Better and best are not measured by affluence; they are measured by destiny.

To the world in which most of us live, money is an aim in itself. It is perceived as carrying with it both power and influence. Yet it does not guarantee either contentment or happiness. Affluence can bring as many problems as it solves. Newspapers are drawing a great deal of attention to those who have become affluent and yet have found their lives thrown into turmoil and unhappiness.

Christians, more than anyone else, need to be clear in their understanding of money. It is not money that is the problem, but the attitude towards it. James writes concerning those who are boastful towards it, plan it and link it into their destiny. Destiny is not like a pension scheme; it is not index-linked. In 1 Timothy 6:10 Paul warns of a danger. The danger is not the possession of wealth, but the love of it. In Luke 12 Jesus gives a similar warning.

The mistake that some make is thinking that only those who have wealth love it. Affluence and money can be a greater problem to those without it than to those with it. Many lives are spent trying to obtain riches, an ambition that can eat away at the destiny of a man.

One mistake that is not uncommon is to assume that financial security is a guarantee of a brighter tomorrow. This gives us some insight into the deceit of riches. For wealth, riches, affluence, or whatever term we use can be a smokescreen to the truth. Few fulfil their destiny by being affluent, but many do by walking away from the desire of affluence.

Take for example some of the disciples, who left what were considered to be reasonable occupations, and the prime example in all things, the Lord Jesus Christ, who being rich became poor for our benefit.

Jesus taught that it was hard for the wealthy to inherit the Kingdom of God. Much of what Jesus had to say was on the issue of wealth, making it abundantly clear that the desire for affluence and pursuit of destiny do not make for easy partners.

We must be clear on one point. God has called us and He desires that we prosper, a truth that does not always appear to be clear to all believers. To be prosperous or to know prosperity is to be enlarged or fulfilled. This sounds very much like being blessed, and no one would deny that right of the believer.

Blessing and affluence though come from different worlds; affluence from this world, blessing from the spiritual. The spiritual man doesn't need evidence of financial security to be fulfilled, nor to be certain of his future, for his trust is in God.

Affluence and the pursuit thereof make a powerful statement. It says it has no need of faith, for it can rely on itself. Yet without faith there are two things we will never do. The first is please God and the second is fulfil our destiny. Faith is a mighty key in unlocking God's almighty power.

Affluence also says that it has control. It creates a sense of independence. Suddenly, nobody else, God included, are deemed to be necessary for life to be sustained. Unfortunately such a life will be largely influenced by the desires of the flesh, for such is the nature of affluence. There is no room for the giver and sustainer of both life and destiny.

We understand that affluence is a deception. It deceives people into believing that material possessions are of greater importance than spiritual principles, and that temporal matters take priority over eternal ones.

It also deceives people into putting possessions in a place of priority over other people. God did not send His Son into the world to save or repair possessions, but to save and to heal people. The early Christians sold their possessions to help others, not as a down payment for better possessions.

People are the currency of God's Kingdom. Spiritual and Ministry Gifts are given for the benefit of people. Desires for affluence sidetrack us into thinking about objects, when we should be thinking about the object of God's affection, people.

Affluence can also deter people from their work. It can make even the industrious lazy. Haggai is a marvellous book with much to say on the subject of wealth. God speaks to His people with a mighty challenge that is as relevant as a warning today as when it was first given. He asks why His house is lying in ruin when His people are living in luxury (Haggai 1:4). God brought His people out of captivity, but they had no concern or desire to restore the Temple. Rather than rebuild a monument to the greatness of God and fulfil their destiny, they sat at home in comfort. Initially we have to ask why many churches struggle financially when their members live in luxury? There is another worrying interpretation of the challenge. God desires that we fulfil our destinies in the building of His house (i.e. the Church), yet many of us sit at home and enjoy the warmth and comfort of our own lives and affluence; not unable, but unwilling to work.

When God calls us to our destiny, He wants to make us conquerors, not comfortable. Our destiny involves putting on the whole armour of God. When Paul lists the armour associated with warfare in Ephesians 6 he does not include slippers and a pipe!

Some live as though their work is ended and they have already entered into their rest. Has God forgotten to call them home, or have they got the sequence wrong? Heaven is our rest; earth is our place of employment.

Along with affluence comes a temptation to feel a sense of permanency on earth. Hebrews 11 makes it clear that we are no more than aliens, pilgrims and strangers here. The earth is the place of our journey, not our destination. Our destiny begins on earth but is completed in heaven.

Only those who accept the temporary nature of our sojourn on earth will be ready for Jesus to return or to call them home. Ninety-nine per cent ready is not enough. Once our destiny grips us we will become homesick for heaven. Only total preparation for the return of Jesus will be enough.

In secular employment I regularly worked 12 hours plus per day, and the harder and longer the day, the more relieved I was to go home. Why are so few of us excited about heaven? Could it be that because it is not tied to our understanding of our destiny, and to our role of working on earth, the concept of going home is lost upon us? Unless we realize we are not at home now, going home will mean nothing to us. Only those who have left the desire for affluence behind will be excited about heaven.

In the same way it is only when we accept our destiny that we can fulfil it. We must not succumb to the errors of rejecting it for self, or replacing it with self. We must accept it for what it is and where it originates. To do so will be to submit to God and His will for our lives, at which point we are ready to experience the glory of His presence and the power of His Spirit. God honours acceptance of destiny.

This level of commitment is made considerably more understandable when we accept the uncertainty of life. James reminds us we cannot be certain we will see tomorrow. We can plan our pensions and our financial investments, and to do so is a matter of human choice, but whether we live to see the investment mature is the prerogative of God and God alone.

As we cannot guarantee ourselves a future, should we not consult with the One in whose hands all our futures are held? This is why the rich man in Luke 12 was a fool. He wasn't a fool because he was rich! He was a fool because he trusted in riches rather than God for his future. If only God controls the future how much wiser it would be to leave it in His hands.

James strengthens his argument by reminding us that life can be as insignificant as a mist that rises and vanishes away. It is hardly noticeable when it rises and is just as quickly gone. Trying to make our mark on time will not see our destiny fulfilled. The very best that will remain after our day is a plaque or a nameplate. Whether it is on the door of a university, hospital, office block or just a headstone matters little in the eternal scheme. They are equal in significance; for all that they bear witness to is that God has summoned an individual to give account of himself.

We can leave an eternal mark. In Hebrews 11:36-38 we see people who fulfilled their destiny on earth, but were neither accepted nor appreciated. Tributes in the world centre around a sense of belonging, and we do not belong. For the Christian, it is more important to receive reward in heaven than tribute on earth.

The God of our destiny is the God who is at the helm of history. It is He who turns its pages; it is He who writes its ending. An ending so mighty that it revolutionizes nations, alters lives and sees His Kingdom come on earth as it already is in heaven; an ending in which He graciously invites us to share. Whether we accept or not is dependent upon what we do about our calling and destiny.

It is sometimes said that some choose greatness while others have it thrust upon them. We have it given us, wrapped in our destiny.

We must also accept the responsibility that such a destiny brings. To not be living in our destiny and calling is to be living outside of the blessing of God. The best in life is tied into our destiny. A destiny which is not to be treated either lightly or as if it were optional. We talk about fulfilling potential as if it doesn't really matter. We think that if a person settles for less than the best it is all right. The truth is that it is disobedience, and that disobedience is sin.

James seeks to make this point abundantly clear. Sin is sin because it is disobedience to God. The man who is morally good, judged to be a role model by his peers, lives according to the Christian standard of his day, but lives outside of his destiny is living outside the plan of God and is therefore guilty of sin. When we know what God wants us to do, and do not do it, we sin.

Some choose to ignore the destiny God has created for them, others are ignorant of it. Either way, we all have to give account of what we do and what we neglect to do. For the one who knows what God expects and does it, a glorious destiny and a crown of righteousness are awaiting.

CHAPTER TWELVE

Seedtime and Harvest

. . . The cries of the harvesters have reached the ears of the Lord Almighty (James 5:4).

When James writes about harvests he is touching on a vitally important subject. For one of the most powerful spiritual principles to be found in the Bible is that of sowing and reaping, or as it is referred to in Genesis 8:22, seedtime and harvest. This is a principle that when it is integrated into the life of a believer will radically transform his outlook and attitude.

It is vital, not least, because it dovetails into our understanding of destiny. Once we grasp the truth about destiny, our whole life opens up like a water lily before us, and integral to that happening, is that what we do and how we act is seen in the light of sowing and reaping.

This is not a subconscious decision-making process, but an understanding of what is going on in our lives. If destiny puts meaning into our lives, then sowing and reaping are a part of the realization and actualization of that destiny.

It is a problem for some Christians that they do not understand their lives, and especially the events that form it. Events that take place bypass their understanding and so there is neither understanding nor appreciation of what is taking place around them. Life becomes more of a meander than a journey.

Yet nothing is accidental. God loves every one of us too much for that to be the case and the fact that He has an eternal plan of which all Christians are a part proves it. Every situation that we find ourselves in is an opportunity to sow or to reap, and often both. While we are sowing today, we are often reaping what we sowed yesterday.

Sowing and reaping are the ways in which we influence our destiny and our spiritual prosperity. Right back in the beginning of Creation God chose a method within nature to bless man. In Genesis 1:11-12,29 God ordains seedtime and harvest as a principle. What you sow is what you reap.

Now we are entering important territory. Territory that is often either avoided altogether or trespassed upon by heresy. Sowing and reaping is not the method of a vindictive divine tyrant to bestow punishment. Physical illness or loss of employment is not God's means of punishment. This principle is above such ideas. Only natural people think on the natural. Spiritual people think and live above that level and see God's love and mercy at work in this and in every such principle.

God gave seed that we might reap a harvest. The talents, gifts and ministries you and I possess are seeds that we sow. The detail of that sowing will determine the type of harvest that we reap. Yet they are not the context of what is written in James 5.

James brings this particular principle to his reader's attention in a powerful way, for he applies it to the use and abuse of finance. As we live in the midst of a materialistic world this is undoubtedly one of the most important issues that face all Christians today. For all its relevance it is still a subject that many are too shy or frightened to face up to.

Is it not strange that when we examine the relevance of the Church today, we discover it has little to say on a subject about which the Bible in general and Jesus in particular has much to say? What compounds the strangeness is that it is an area of great confusion that remains largely ignored.

James does not dodge the issue, but in fact meets it head-on, and does so in the light of this great spiritual principle. He is writing to people who have financial problems, but that does not mean they do not have money. It simply means they have problems. We have seen that too often we try to solve problems without addressing the actual problem, but by addressing peripheral issues. The problem was not the wealth, but a lack of understanding of how to use it and what to do with it. James has some valuable instruction for us.

We see the cry of the harvesters. People are affected by how we live our lives, spend our money, and sow our seed. We are not the only ones who are affected by our harvest. Others are affected, and this must influence our financial decisions. What do the harvesters cry out? What do they have to say? The cry is a condemnation of the nature of the harvest. In James 5:4 we are told that the cry of the unpaid wages finds its way into the ears of the Lord of the Harvest.

When we have to give an account of ourselves before God, if we have used our finances unwisely, there will be no need of a lawyer or barrister for the prosecution. The harvest that results from what we have sown will testify against us.

The first factor that James highlights as determining our harvest is the timing of when we sow. He makes it clear that those to whom he is writing had hoarded their wealth. They had kept their money and therefore their seed to themselves. The most obvious aspect of sowing and reaping is that without a seedtime there is no harvest. This is a simple point, but it is a very serious point. When we give our tithes and offering is important. It should be based upon the principle of seedtime, not on the principle of convenience.

Almost every year I intend to save money by planting seeds in my greenhouse, so that my wife Paula and I will not have to spend a small fortune on plants to ornate our pots and hanging baskets come springtime. Every year I leave it too late and a subsequent visit to local Garden Centres costs more than I care to admit. If we do not sow in time for a harvest, we cannot expect one. Our giving should not be based on what is left over, but the first 'fruits' or seed that we receive.

The time of sowing determines whether plants flower early or late, whether they will be protected from the elements and even whether they will flower at all.

The first year that I was a student in Bible College I had no visible means of support. I relied upon God to meet all the financial requirements such as fees and the cost of accommodation. I made a decision, that if God wanted me to stay He would have to supply the money. It was He who called me to go, He would meet my need.

There were many miracles that took place, but one in particular always blesses me when I recall it. A lady hundreds of miles away had been diagnosed as having cancer, and had set aside a sum of money in preparation for her funeral. In the meantime God undertook for her physical need. Then another miracle took place, for on realizing she did not need the money for her funeral she felt in her heart that she should send it to me. What she did not know was that at that particular time I had a specific need to be met in that the payment of the next term's fees was due.

When I relate this and similar stories people sometimes give the impression of jealousy. It is as though living by 'faith' as it is sometimes called is a privilege for a select few. Firstly it isn't for the select few, but it is a privilege. It is the living-out of the principle of seedtime and harvest. Whatever our means of support, we reap what we have sown. If we do not give, our harvest will dry up.

The blessing of giving is greater than receiving. To see God answer your prayer and provide for you is great, but to sow into another person's life and ministry is even greater.

The natural man is happy to harvest another man's crops, but the spiritual man is happier sowing in another man's field. If you find yourself jealous of another man's ministry, sow into it and share in its harvest. Give time and money to it. Encourage it and tell others about it. Then you will not harvest in bitterness but in rejoicing.

One of the reasons that some churches in this nation have failed to reap for many generations is because they have not sown. Apart from overheads and administration costs of running the local church, for every nine people who tithe (give a tenth of their income) we should be able to release a labourer into the harvest (assuming he tithes!). Yet our nation sees very few full-time Christian workers, and churches that should have full-time workers do not. We owe it to our children, youth, pensioners, new converts, students, the homeless, the infirm, the lonely etc. to release new ministries and help into their midst. If we withhold our seed, there will be no harvest.

If we have a concern for our nation we must sow! If we do not work at this point of time, our seedtime, we will not know a harvest. We have already seen that the Early Church sold their possessions, but they did so in order to have the money ready to sow into the need as soon as it arose. You do not react to seedtime, you plan for it. Notice Paul writes in 1 Corinthians 16:2 to put aside money for those in need, ready to be used. To use the words of the world, we attempt to put the cart before the horse, or to use the words of a spiritual principle, we seek to put the harvest before the seedtime.

From the personal point of the sower, note how the seed was hoarded. It was not sown. Wealth turns into waste unless it is ploughed back into the Kingdom of God. Seeds not sown are wasted. Wealth that is not re-sown is seed that is gone to waste.

In 2 Corinthians 9:10 Paul writes of a harvest of righteousness that is reaped from the seeds of money. A strange connection? Certainly not! Withholding seed from the Kingdom of God leads to a poor harvest or no harvest at all. Remember Haggai 1 where people had little because they sowed unwisely, and what they did have was of no blessing to them. Having returned to their homeland at a time of sowing, they failed to sow good seed.

Sowing your money into the harvest fields of God will bring a spiritual harvest, because the greater blessing rests with the hand that gives rather than with the hand that receives. This is why there are Christians whose spiritual growth has become stunted. They have not sown. To sow is to exercise faith and love, without which at the very forefront of our lives, we cannot expect either blessing or growth.

When or whether we sow is a vital fact, but no less important is where we sow. For where we sow will have a determining effect upon our harvest. In James 5:1 there were those who were already awaiting an awful harvest, a harvest of judgement. This was not because of a judgmental or merciless God, but because they had sown their seed in the natural not in the spiritual realm.

Self-indulgence does not produce a profitable or a palatable harvest. A gardener who grows plants for the love of plants will produce better quality plants than one who grows only for what he can take out.

God does not give gifts to men for personal aggrandizement, nor does He give finance for such a purpose. Yet for all that, the choice of where we sow is entirely ours. This is why both the harvest and the harvesters can testify against us. It is our decision, our duty, our destiny and our responsibility.

We have a clear example of this in the New Testament with Ananias and Sapphira. They sold some land and gave a part of the money to help the poor. They kept back a part of the money, but claimed they had given it all. In Acts 5:3-4 we have the record of Peter speaking to Ananias. What he has to say is of great importance to us; for the land before it was sold belonged to Ananias. The choice of how much would be given away belonged to Ananias. The sin lay in the lies and deceit, not in the partial gift.

Ananias sowed to the flesh. His financial adviser was his ego and consequently his advice was deeply flawed. Paul writes the following words in Galatians 6:8 'The one who sows to please his sinful nature, from that nature will reap destruction; the one who sows to please the Spirit, from the Spirit will reap eternal life.'

If we sow to our pleasure we will reap judgement, if we sow to God's pleasure we will know blessing and a bountiful life.

Now we find ourselves at an important stage of our thinking. It may be that some of the things that we highlight to the unsaved we fail to recognize ourselves. We fill our sermons with the folly of materialism, yet still endeavour to live materialistic lives.

We all have the choice to invest our money in financial institutions in the hope and desire of financial security; yet the best we can expect to reap is financial reward on earth. If we invest our money in the Kingdom of God we will know financial security on earth, a fulfilled and abundant life, joy and contentment and a hope that shines into eternity. In addition to all those things we will receive a reward in heaven. The choice lies with each and every one of us.

What we should be aware of is the disillusionment that comes to those who desire a spiritual harvest but are only prepared to sow to the sinful nature. We must make a conscious decision that governs where the harvest will be. The time to decide is at seedtime, but too many believers try to decide later. If you plant cabbage seed, all the positive thinking or wishing in the world will not allow you to reap onions. If you want onions, plant onions; but decide at seedtime, not at harvest.

The Christian that does not sow what he wants to reap is a very discontented and unfulfilled person. If we want to fulfil our destiny in God we must sow our seed into that destiny, not into what earthly wisdom advises. Rather than sow into self-indulgence we must sow into ministries and needs that will produce for us a good and righteous harvest.

We must be mindful too that how we sow determines our harvest. The Lord Almighty hears the cries of unpaid bills or wages that testify against us. He heard the cry of the outstanding balance that Ananias claimed to have sown into the work of God. We do not need to boast, the seed and the harvest speak for themselves. We must therefore sow justly.

This is a crucial aspect of how we should sow. If we want a harvest of righteousness, we must sow in righteousness. We are not investing for natural reward, and God does not honour dishonour. The old Pentecostal Fathers in Wales spoke of keeping short accounts and leaving no debts outstanding. They did not wait for reminders; they paid their bills on time, or earlier. Why? Because God is no man's debtor and it was a testimony to the world of the provision of God.

Being a child of God is not an opportunity to exploit others financially. God is a God of justice and integrity, and He expects us to deal with all men in a similar manner. Some teach that because Christ has conquered the prince of this world, we can pillage it and take what we want. This is a dangerous attitude. Firstly how much of this world do we want, and why? Secondly read very carefully the account of the Children of Israel leaving Egypt. In Exodus 11:2-3 we read that they were to ask the Egyptians for the possessions they wanted. This was their due. This was the result of the cry of the harvesters reaching the ears of the Lord Almighty. They were collecting what they were owed for their servitude. God laid up the wealth of Egypt for His people, but they did not steal it! God touched the hearts of the Egyptians and made them favourably disposed to His people. This is important for when we deal with the world as individuals and as churches we can expect God to lower prices and perform miracles providing what is expensive freely, but it is the result of God's influence upon the people we deal with. It is not the result of fraud, theft, manipulation or the taking advantage of people. Our sowing must be in honesty, integrity and righteousness.

Israel knew defeat at Ai (Joshua 7) because Achan put possessions before obedience. We must sow in obedience, for disobedience does not produce a good harvest. There are Christians who live in defeat both spiritually and financially because there are outstanding debts that have not been dealt with. They have been disobedient in their financial dealings. As Christians we should be the easiest people to deal with financially; though sadly this is not always the case.

Some live impoverished lives because they sow sparingly. To sow sparingly is to waste. The principle of the wealth that God gives is 'use it or lose it'. People who amass money and sow sparingly are not to be admired or held up as role models. Such people live weak and unfulfilled lives, insofar as they cannot reach their destiny. The many that sow abundantly reap abundantly. Like begets like, that is the law of the harvest. Little begets little, much begets much.

I like the story of the old Pentecostal preacher who pastored a small church that could not afford to pay him a salary. It was decided that he would be allowed to keep all that went into the offering. After a while he noticed a trend; the more he put in, the more he had back! If he put in an extra pound he got an extra pound. While the example is a simple one, the principle is true. The more we put in, the more we receive back. It was not long before that preacher was getting more than a pound back for every pound he put in. What might appear natural can be spiritual if we allow the seed time to germinate. Remember it's the fruit of the harvest that reveals the truth of the seed.

Wealth that is not sown becomes corrupt. James writes of gold that has become corroded. This is interesting because gold is the symbol of all that the world looks for in wealth. Precious, highly sought after and valued, and of course a symbol of security. Yet the best of material wealth if it is not sown becomes spiritually corroded.

We should remember that it is not only what you sow but what you do not sow that is important. We must sow everything we can. This is the way that the first Christians sowed, and they knew mighty blessing. They did not know everything and they were far from perfect, but they knew how to sow. It is with this in mind that James is so critical of those who sow both sparingly and selfishly.

When we are deciding how much to sow, perhaps we should consider the effect on the seed that is left behind. Jesus commended a widow who gave only a little, because she gave out of her poverty. She sowed good seed. What will He say about our seed and us?

In 2 Corinthians 9:7 we are reminded that '. . . God loves a cheerful giver.' We must not sow with reluctance but with desire. Only those who understand destiny can understand the desire to sow into the spiritual. Only such an understanding can be encouraged to give with joy into the Kingdom of God. This is not an exercise in how to ease the conscience, or that gives a feel-good factor at helping others. It is the realization that we are a part of the greatest plan in the history of the world and can sow our money as well as our lives into it.

Can we sow money into the Kingdom of God, believing that the needy will be ministered to and the lost led to Christ and not rejoice? There is a tremendous realization that money cannot buy salvation, but that sown in faith it can contribute to the setting free of a man from his burden of sin and deliver him from the power of evil. This realization should cause the most sober and traditionally formal of us to throw our hats into the air and praise God.

To exercise faith is more than important, it is vital. To give is more than important, again it is vital. To give in faith is miraculous in its power. It is one way that we can unlock the mighty demonstration of God's power in the lives of our friends, family, churches and our nation. We do not need to pray to see if we should give, we should give. Once sown, we pray the Lord of the Harvest to give the increase.

Giving is a thrilling way to unlock power within our lives. It is a principle and a pattern of living. We must not miss out on this vital part of our lives. Let us give!

CHAPTER THIRTEEN

The Practice of Patience

Be patient, then, brothers, until the Lord's coming . . .
(James 5:7).

Of all the traits and characteristics that are missing in Britain today, near the top must come patience. There are whole industries built upon the need to cater for lack of this virtue. We have everything instant. There is instant tea, coffee, meals, loans, and mortgages. In fact if you look hard enough almost anything you could want is available in an instant. You may have affluence, you may have success, you may have friends, but the chances are you do not have time. Everything is so speeded up that life is lived at a frantic pace. Unless it is, the assumption is made that life is boring.

We must be careful that we do not become ensnared in this spider's web of deceit. The nearer the Lord's return, the worse it will become. The enemy of our souls seeks to sidetrack us from God's plan by speeding up life to such a pace that we lose our priorities.

For a number of successive years I competed in an annual 10K athletics race. It started on the side of a mountain with the first kilometre downhill. Then one year I rather ambitiously started at the front of the competitors, and found myself out in the front and unable to slow down because those behind were pushing the pace, and me with it. I went through the first kilometre almost a minute faster than previous years, yet recorded a slower time. When it came time to climb back up the mountain and the competitors slowed down, old men walking their dogs were going past me. The problem was that I ran at a pace dictated by others and lost sight of my race plan.

It is no surprise that the writer to the Hebrews (12:1) advises us to run patiently the race we have been called to run. Without patience we lose sight of our calling and destiny. Even though we know we are called to run our own race it is still a temptation to let others dictate the pace.

If we learn from seedtime and harvest we will learn that everything has its appointed time and season. To fulfil our destiny and become mature as Christians we must live in the truth of this principle and understand that patience leads to godliness. Godliness cannot be forced and it cannot be rushed. It is a process of maturing. Mushrooms spring up overnight, but oak trees take many years to mature. The depth of our experience in God will be in line with our patience. How often we pray for patience and demand it now!

We also see from Hebrews 6:12 that patience is essential to the man who wants to inherit what has been promised to him. No patience, no destiny. It is not conditional, nor is it optional. Patience is an integral part of living life the way Christ intended it to be lived. We should live according to the divine timetable, not according to ours.

We must note that true godliness is not instant, nor is being made into the likeness of Jesus. It is a lifelong process that does not reach completion until we reach our eternal destiny. With this in mind James moves along his sequence of instruction and enlarges upon the subject of destiny by raising the importance of patience. This he does in 5:7-11 and shows us the three key elements of patience, anticipation, tolerance and perseverance.

Once again we return to sowing and reaping. If we sow the right attitudes in our hearts, minds and lives we will reap patience.

As we consider these points we realize that patience does not just come down from heaven and mystically alight upon us. It is the right alignment of all that we are. Our thoughts, hopes and desires all need to be linked to and aligned with God's plan and our destiny. We do not choose to be either patient or impatient. If we think we can, we fool ourselves; but we are able to influence the factors that go to determine whether patience reigns within our hearts and minds. One such factor is anticipation; an attitude we should constantly be aware should be at the forefront of our minds. Without anticipation there can be no patience.

Destiny understands that the process of its fulfilment is continual, but its finality is greater than that very process itself. James urges Christians to anticipate the Lord's return to earth. This is the ultimate destiny of which our destinies are a part. The man who is patient is prepared to wait because of what he anticipates and the fact he anticipates it.

Patience develops hope. How? The answer is not only simple but deeply profound. True patience anticipates what is yet to happen. It is the seedtime of what is harvested as hope.

James gives an example in keeping with the agricultural theme of seedtime and harvest. The farmer sows his seed, and although there may be little sign of rain and even less sign of a harvest, yet he is patiently anticipating what he hopes will be a valuable crop. While he waits, he rehearses in his mind how he will organize the reaping. This is a time of eager anticipation. James identifies the two main periods of rainfall as the autumn and the spring rains. The spring rain comes just before the time of harvest, when the grain would be maturing. The farmer, based upon a mixture of understanding and experience, patiently awaits the rain and the ensuing harvest, yet it is still to arrive.

James exhorts his readers to adopt a similar attitude of anticipation; an encouragement that we would do well to heed today. I cannot imagine any man living for God and His purposes in our generation, making a significant impact and not living in the anticipation of the Lord's return. To make a mark upon our nation we will need to have a great love for the Saviour, and if we possess that we will welcome and anticipate His return.

There is an old saying that suggests our lives should be lived as if it were yesterday Jesus died, today He had risen and tomorrow He will return. Everything that is taking place is so in readiness for His return. The great political leaders and decision-makers are, whether they know it or not, a part of the Master's master plan. Our attitude and expression should be one of great anticipation for that great and triumphant day. It should grip our lives, work and ministry to know that we are willingly a part of such a plan.

Such longing will be based upon the two key elements of anticipation that make patience possible. Firstly expectation and secondly desire.

The Christian builds his anticipation on expectation. This carries with it the idea of excitement. Patience is neither boring nor negative, and it is certainly not the almost fatalistic acceptance of what befalls us in life that some believe it to be.

Some picture it in their minds as just waiting, passively killing time until circumstances change, or maybe just waiting for chance. This could not be further from the truth. Anticipation and expectation are vibrant and exciting. True patience excites the heart as it ponders what it waits for in God.

God does not lie. What He has promised will come about. Our experience from the very day of conversion until the present day tells us that God is a God that honours His Word and His promises, and that His plan for this world could never come to completion unless Jesus returns. The return of Jesus is still this world's destiny.

The second aspect or element of anticipation is desire. Only

THE PRACTICE OF PATIENCE

what we desire will we anticipate. If an event is looming that we
dread, we do not wait for it with patience, but with fear. The
farmer desires a wonderful crop and in accordance with that
desire has a wonderful anticipation.

This leaves us with an important conclusion to draw. Only
those whose desire is in line with their destiny can know true
patience. Otherwise there is little basis on which to build
expectation and feed desire. If what we anticipate feeds the flesh
and not the spirit, we will feed impatience, but if what we
anticipate feeds the spirit we will develop patience.

We see too that patience is tolerant of others. If patience is a
virtue missing from society today, then the greatest evidence of
its absence must be intolerance of others. Peer pressure does not
only exist in certain groups within society, such as teenagers and
children. There is a general intolerance of anyone that is
different or challenges the accepted standard that society has set
for itself.

Christians must be tolerant. Jesus was. He stood against
injustice and wrong, speaking out boldly and loudly against it.
That however, is vastly different to speaking out against those
whose only wrong is to see things differently, speak differently,
or even look different to you. We saw in the warning against
showing favouritism, that partiality is not a doctrine on which
the Bible teaches we should stand firm. Yet how many
Christians have switched off from listening to a preacher
because of personal views? Perhaps his shoes were dirty, his hair
too long, his tie too loud or some other embarrassingly petty
observation. Far too often judgements are made about people on
evidence that bears no relevance or value.

On this matter James returns to the principle of seedtime and
harvest. Those who sow judgement, reap judgement. Yet those
who are the most intolerant are often the very ones who expect
others to be tolerant of them.

James returns to another former and recurring subject, control and use of the tongue. Christians are not to be grumblers. Grumblers do not stand on big issues, but jump up and down over the more insignificant of matters.

As a young man contemplating Christian Ministry, I was given some sound advice by an experienced pastor. Like many profound sayings it was very simple. The advice was to be a little man on little issues but a big man on big issues. We have no place in being dogmatic on issues of no great importance. We should shrink out of sight when the insignificant is being debated, but we should stand to the point of death when it comes to eternal matters.

Is it not the case that grumbling between Christians often starts over the most insignificant of matters? Arguments over colour schemes and parking spaces cause people to be outspoken, while heresy and poor teaching go unchallenged.

Here James uses a word that has a deeper meaning than just grumbling. It conveys the idea of an inner groaning, that does not necessarily need to be uttered. It may be felt as much as spoken.

The patient believer does not become personally disillusioned or embittered by what he sees in other people and their actions. When a person backslides the reasons presented are often not the real causes, but reasons easier to defend than the true one. The original reasons usually relate back not to what somebody else may have done or said, but the reaction to it. There is a big difference.

I may see a fellow Christian doing something that is generally accepted as being unbecoming of a Christian, and human nature being what it is, I will naturally have an opinion on his actions. I do not have to approve of his actions, but neither do I have to be intolerant of him. If I wish to speak with him or discuss it with leaders of my church it may be my right, but if I feel resentment towards him, that is my responsibility not his. I could take the time to find out the truth, not what I perceive it to be, but I must ensure that bitterness or anger does not cause me to fall out of communion with him and with God.

Patience isn't about ignoring sin or letting it go as if it were of no importance, yet it comes first to the man whose mind is concentrated on putting himself right with God, whatever it takes and however long that might be.

It might sound a bit too simplistic to say that the patient man is not impatient with others, but it is true and sometimes overlooked. In 1 Corinthians 13:4 patience is identified as a characteristic of love. We cannot be intolerant of others and love them at the same time. While it is true that we need to be patient with ourselves, because God has yet to finish His work in us, we must always remember that the same is equally true of others.

James highlights the need of patience in suffering. The believer may have much to tempt him and try him, but he is in good company. Take the example given; Job and the prophets. They have left a legacy to the world that is above monetary value. Their legacy is spiritual, the example of righteousness in general and patience in particular.

In contemporary use today the words patience and perseverance are often used interchangeably, but in James there is a subtle difference in the way they are used. Patience carries the idea of continuing unchanged whereas perseverance conveys the more specific idea of standing against opposition. This latter description could certainly be said of Job and the heroes of old.

It may well be that the greatest evidence and proving ground of patience is perseverance. This is one of the reasons that God still allows Christians to experience real opposition from the world. Opposition, persecution, suffering, perseverance and patience are not theories, but real and tangible. Only real opposition can lead to real perseverance. Paul exhorts us all in Romans 5:3-4 concerning the value of suffering. It contributes to our spiritual growth. The words he wrote are important to believers today, '. . . we also rejoice in our sufferings, because we know that suffering produces perseverance; perseverance, character; and character, hope.'

James touched on this subject earlier in chapter 1 with regard to the trial of our faith. It is not the circumstances but the attitudes that prevail in the circumstances and the actions that come out of them that produce good fruit.

We have seen earlier too, that God does not allow circumstances to enter our lives that we might know failure and defeat, but that we might know success and victory. Suffering is an experience that to the natural man is seen as a setback, but to the spiritual man it is an opportunity to prove God.

Having established this as a principle within his life the Christian should persevere because he is a man who believes. The prophets did not just speak in the Name of the Lord, they believed in Him.

During my student days I spent enough time waiting on railway platforms to last me several lifetimes, but out of the boredom and frustration at least one good thing emerged. A lesson was learned. However late the hour, however distant the station and however overdue the train, dismay did not replace perseverance until I stopped believing the train was actually on its way.

Whatever degree of suffering or hardship we are undergoing, the key is not our circumstances, but our faith. If we believe that God is merciful and full of compassion, we will endure and persevere. Once we stop believing in God as He is, and our destiny in Him, then our ability to persevere even the slightest obstacle will be impaired. When we stop believing that there is actually a train on the way we will start to look for alternative forms of transport. From then on, doubt will start to wreak its own particular forms of havoc.

We should also see that the man who perseveres is a man who is blessed. No Christian can know a blessed life unless they are experiencing victory. Unless we know perseverance we will know only defeat. It is victory over the evil one and what others would deem to be adverse circumstances that makes us whole and fulfilled. We can never be complete without such victories, for victory is our destiny, it is what God has chosen for us.

As we read through Hebrews 11 we see the 'Hall of Fame' of the 'Heroes of Faith' and cannot help but notice that not all found deliverance in this life, but their perseverance took them to a greater crown than can be worn this side of eternity. The great characters of the Bible have proven to be great role models of victory over adversity, and two of the characteristics that stand out is that they did it through God's strength and perseverance.

What of us and our role models? Those who triumph in pain, those who are victorious in the heat of battle are the very ones whose lives and encouragement drive us to a deeper relationship in God. We should follow the example of such people, but we should also be seeking to be our generation's role models.

Our nation, locality, family, friends and work colleagues alike will not be won to Jesus unless they see in us the things we see in people like Job. To show others Jesus we must first make Him visible in our lives. Perseverance and patience in hostile situations or in suffering can be as powerful a testimony as the miraculous.

If we are to leave a legacy to the world, and that legacy is to be of any spiritual and eternal value, it must involve both perseverance and patience. To fail in this regard is to fail to follow in the footsteps of Jesus and to fail in fulfilling our destiny in God. To sow good seed, and see that seed turn into a good harvest we must wait with patience.

CHAPTER FOURTEEN

Effective Prayer

. . . The prayer of a righteous man is powerful and effective (James 5:16).

It must be wholly without grounds for controversy that any work on the Christian's life and calling would be incomplete unless it at least touched on prayer. Therefore it is hardly surprising that James should want to bring such an important subject to the attention of his readers. For if the finished work of Christ is the basis of a relationship with God, then prayer is the means of sustaining it. It is an integral part of the growth process within the life of every believer.

Yet for all the sermons, books and discussion on prayer and all the prayers prayed, the effects too rarely measure up to those of the prayers of men like Elijah. This is not a fact that should be either ignored or explained away with unsatisfactory answers that do not face the very heart of the matter. There is doubtless a multiplicity of reasons as to why revival tarries in Great Britain, but a willingness to avoid the issue of ineffective prayer must surely figure high on that list.

The truth is, there has been less than enough meaningful teaching on the matter, and this unexplained willingness to avoid facing up to the issue. Too many people accept unanswered prayer as the norm and answers to prayer as the exception. To make matters worse, we exaggerate or claim what is not an answer to prayer to be one. Something born out of enthusiasm, but not wisdom. With such points in our mind, can we really wonder why the world is sceptical about prayer, and many Christians fail to understand it?

We preach that there is no substitute and no alternative to prayer, yet we act differently. We are always looking for new ways, alternative methods and different ministries when often what we have to do is stop and pray effectively. There is a great price to be paid for neglect of prayer. Unfortunately churches generally and Christians more specifically have paid that price. A price that includes a great loss of blessing.

To see God move in our lives and nation we must come to terms with the truth about prayer. Unless we deal with this matter in an honest and sincere manner we will not see the demonstration of God's power. We must be aware too, that although God's power is almighty and without restrictions, it is not without conditions that we see it moving in our Christian life.

God's plan for the Christian's life is undoubtedly to answer prayer. He does not encourage us to ask of Him that He might turn us down. He does not exhort us to speak in order to turn a deaf ear. He does not command us to pray that He might ignore us. God's desire for every believer is that they might have communion with Him, in a manner that includes communication. Prayer is the believer's vital breath, its worth beyond human estimation.

So great is its importance that at first glance it seems a little strange that James does not deal with prayer earlier. Having made reference to its importance and noting its obvious relevance to all Christians, why does he raise other issues before he teaches on prayer? The answer lies not in what many understand prayer to be, but what James sees as effective prayer.

James is not encouraging people to speak to God and list requests, but to obtain promises, move obstacles, challenge and overcome the laws of nature and touch lives, changing them forever. This is powerful, history shaping, destiny forming prayer.

Such prayer as James is referring to, will come as a result of the issues he has faithfully presented before us. Often we preach that holiness and righteousness come only as an answer to prayer. This is not entirely true and is something of an excuse for lack of obedience to God. We should be preaching that such things come to a person as a result of obedience to God's Word, and that answers to prayer come as a result of righteousness and holiness. The life that knows answers to prayer is a life that is spiritually ordered before God.

We should be putting our lives right before God in order to pray. Prayers of faith come from hearts of faith, not lives of sin. Prayer should not be an end in itself. It matters what we say, why we say it and whether or not the prayer is answered. It matters to God, it matters to those in need, and it should matter to us.

We should not only make time for prayer, but we should ensure that we are prepared for prayer. James helps us in this regard with some powerful and challenging, yet clear and concise instruction.

I am sure we have all heard preachers refer to the place of prayer, though usually they are referring to the physical location. We make much of this particular sideline, when a sideline is what it is. Men with a desire to pray will find a place to pray, even in a crowd, while those with either no or little desire will always find an excuse. Usually it involves not being able to find somewhere to pray! Of course having a private place to go where there are no distractions or interruptions is good, but it is not vital.

More important by far than the place we pray, is the place of prayer within our lives. This is important to James and it should be important to us. We make too much of the location and not enough of the desire. Putting a Christian in a soundproof and locked room with no interruptions and panoramic views of God's handiwork is still no guarantee of answered prayer. Take a

156

man like Elijah, no apparent ease or luxury and his prayers shake a nation, alter the weather patterns and discredit the prophets of a false god in the most powerful way imaginable. Elijah's prayers owed little to the location but everything to the place of prayer in the prophet's life.

When I talk about theology, I like to talk about babies and bath water. The reason being, that when it comes to interpreting the Bible, one of the great dangers is throwing out the baby with the bath water. Too often we dismiss a subject without seeing the important principle. Prayer is such an obvious example. There are those who have specific ministries in supplication and intercession, but to deny the place of such prayer in the life of every believer is to make a terrible mistake.

Prayer should be constantly on our breath. Throughout the New Testament we are encouraged to pray always, and without ceasing. Jesus taught His disciples to pray, and those that went on to write or influence the writings of the New Testament carried on such teaching.

It is impossible to read through the New Testament without appreciating that there is never a time that it is not appropriate to pray. James takes this principle a step further, and shows that not only is there never a time, but even more importantly there are never circumstances that could ever befall us when prayer is not appropriate.

We should distinguish between two words and their inference; necessary and appropriate. Too many only pray when they feel it is necessary. Necessity speaks of a need. Put another way, they have a need themselves. For James prayer is always appropriate, irrespective of need. There is never a time, irrespective of circumstances, when it is not right to communicate with God.

To believe that God is a God that hears and speaks is not enough to understand prayer. We also have to believe that He desires to share in our lives. Prayer is not our opportunity to groan at God about our disgruntled lives and tell Him how to run the country, the lives of others or even His Church. It is for us to share our highs, our lows, our feelings and our emotions. Through prayer God shares in our lives at their deepest and their shallowest parts.

God wants to share in our joy, which is one of the reasons we should sing to Him songs of praise and rejoicing as well as songs of worship and adoration. He wants to share in our petitions; that is why bringing our petitions is right. He wants to deal with our sickness, which is one of the reasons why Jesus died.

To sum this up more succinctly, God should be our first aid and not our last resort. It isn't wrong to have prayer meetings to ask God to intervene and change things that have gone wrong, but prayer should also be proactive as well as reactive.

If prayer is in the right place in a believer's life it will be more than a means of being bailed out of trouble. It will be the means of influencing people and circumstances for the good of God's Kingdom.

Once we have established the importance of the place of prayer in our lives, we must consider the power of prayer. Its immense power is seen in that it can unleash the mighty power of God into our lives and circumstances. Again James touches something of a raw nerve; a point overlooked by some and conveniently ignored by others. He attributes healing and acts of great power to prayer itself. Some argue that it is not prayer but God that performs miracles. We are back to babies and bath water! It is God that performs the miracle, but it is the prayer that causes God to perform it. It is clear in the context that James writes that without the prayer no miracle would take place. A fact from which we can rightly conclude that there are those suffering because effective prayers by righteous people are not ascending heavenward.

If you have ever had the privilege to attend a top class

athletics meeting, you will without doubt have been amazed by the performances of the throwers. These athletes are rarely seen on the television coverage, and when they are it is difficult to appreciate the enormity of their feats. These stars, the great and the huge, mostly well over six feet tall and often weighing upwards of twenty stone move across the ground like lightning, hurling various shaped implements enormous distances. Obviously heavily muscled and at the peak of fitness, they perform these awesome feats not just because they have great strength, but because a minute nerve carries a message to and from the brain. Without strength they could not throw great distances, but without the minute nerve they could not throw at all.

Prayer is like that nerve. It unlocks the power of a mighty and sovereign God. It makes great power within our lives possible. The Christian that lacks power lacks prayer. We must not walk away from the challenge of what James is saying. If we are genuinely spending time in prayer and we are not seeing the power of God, being released in our lives, we must ask of ourselves and of God some very serious questions.

As we ponder the need of our nation we desperately need to see the power of God healing the sick. That this is true is obvious, but we should consider the other example of powerful prayer that James gives.

Elijah was like us, suffering the frailty of humanity. Though, whatever his faults and failings were, he did see fantastic answers to prayer. This ought not to surprise us, for if you sow big requests you get big answers.

I remember an old minister telling me a story of a friend of his, whom while preaching at a particular church had asked for those who were sick to make a line at the front of the hall that he might pray for them. As they were lining up he started to pray for them one by one, but as he was working his way down the line, he noticed the man at the far end of the line only had one leg. Eventually he reached him, by which time he had become quite nervous, and his heart was beating considerably more quickly than was normal and probably more quickly than was healthy. He looked at the man in fear and trembling, but before he could utter a word the man with the one leg explained he had a cold and would like to be prayed for.

I cannot say hand on heart, that I would be any less relieved than the minister in the illustration, but if we only ask for minor ailments to be healed, minor ailments will be the only healing we will ever see. What we sow is, yes, you've guessed it, what we reap. The issue here is a vital one for today's Church to face. Powerful prayers get powerful answers. The power that is sadly lacking in many churches is linked to powerless and ineffective praying.

Elijah's prayer was both powerful and effective. Such prayers are measured by their effectiveness, not by the noise level or facial expressions of intensity. True prayer delivers results.

We must stop hiding behind the sovereignty of God. If our prayers are not answered, we assume it couldn't have been our fault. We assume God in His sovereignty must have overruled us, because it was not His will or desire. This view fits fine with those who have a rigid and unfeeling view of a God that shows neither mercy nor compassion.

Yet such a view ignores the Bible's teaching on the subject. It is also pharisaic in nature and does not do justice to a merciful and compassionate God. Furthermore it leaves those who are burdened with bigger burdens. It leaves those who are ill with a God who is capable of healing them, but they do not know if He wants to.

Prayer is the way God has chosen to share His power with us. A power that is both real and effective. Prayer must be real, tangible, and relate to specific needs in specific lives that the power of God might be directed to personal needs. If we believe this we will pray informed and relevant prayers. When we sow in such a manner we will receive informed and relevant answers.

The ultimate truth that we have just touched on is that it is not about theory. Something that was said to me many years ago sticks in my mind. I have forgotten who said it or where they said it, but it still influences my view of prayer. What was said concerned the great Welsh preachers of the past. It was that they knew nothing of the theology or the theory of prayer, they just prayed. Yet when they just prayed, God would just answer.

Only prayer can bring the amazing into the mundane, and such prayer can only come about by praying. A prayer is not a prayer until it's prayed. Please ponder the meaning of this for just a moment. Prayers have no other value than as prayers. Thoughts and intentions do not heal the sick, but prayer does.

We have seen the importance of our lives being right with God, and James reminds us again here. It is the prayers of the righteous that are powerful and effective. Some place emphasis upon the oratory and language of praying, others on planning the construction of the prayer. The truth is that while none of that is necessary, it is vital we check our hearts and our lives for righteousness. Righteousness is about being right with God, and effective prayers come not from right diction but right attitudes, right hearts and right destinies.

Confession is an important weapon in the armoury of a prayer warrior. It enables us to keep ourselves clean and pure before God. It enables us to keep the channels of prayer open and clear. It is preparing the seed and the soil for a healthy harvest.

Unforgiveness and sin block answers to prayer, like little else on earth. Satan and his demons cannot block the answers to our prayers, but sin can. They cannot prevent God from hearing and answering our prayer, but sin and especially an unforgiving spirit will hamper our relationship with God and cause prayers to go unanswered.

James is not advocating confession in the sense of a priest forgiving sin, but the practice of believers sharing their needs together and ministering into each other's lives. We must keep our relationship with God and with each other both clean and clear at all times. This must be a matter of priority within our lives.

We must observe too the importance of both obedience and submission, areas we have looked at in some detail previously. James illustrates the importance again, by giving the example of elders of the church praying for the sick and anointing them with oil. God does not require help to heal. He does not require us to carry out rituals to make it easier for Him, but He does desire that we prove our obedience and submission.

Before we see answers to prayer, we must be both obedient and submissive. Prayer is mightily powerful as we have already noted, but it is not our means of dictating to God. We must come humbly in submission, recognizing the One with whom it is we are dealing.

We should also see that Elijah prayed earnestly. The more literal translation is that he 'prayed with prayer'. This is interesting to note because it opens up the meaning and the sense of the message that James is conveying. Elijah prayed prayer, not words, monologues or speeches. As with the old Welsh preachers, Elijah just prayed and God just answered.

James having already warned us about the dangers of being double-minded now exhorts us to be single-minded. Elijah was single-minded in his prayer, nothing wavering, no conditions or exceptions. He knew what to ask for, and he asked it. Prayer ceases to be true prayer when it is no longer single-minded in its intention or purpose. There should be no doubt in either what we pray or how we pray. This is an important key to understanding earnest praying.

We saw in James 2 the importance of faith. Here in regard to prayer we see it once again. To be powerful and effective, prayer must be born out of faith. What is the purpose of coming to God in prayer and not believing that He exists, or that He is what He says He is? If it is impossible to please God without faith, the faithless prayer is never going to see an impact made.

Effective praying and prayer ministries are not going to fall into our lap while we are asleep. They are going to grow out of our lives, but only if those lives are grounded in faith and righteousness.

It is also appropriate that James raises this issue where he does. All the other areas of our lives need to be right before God, before we can see the fruit of effective prayer. This does not mean we have to earn the right to be heard, nor does it mean we are heard according to the amount of good works performed. Just the opposite. Our hearts must be right or put right in order to approach God, not in order to earn the right to approach Him.

If we are to fulfil our destiny in God and see His purpose come about within our lives and the nation, then we must return to prayer that is effective. Much of this world's destiny lies within the hands of those who pray. Dependent upon the way we practice prayer will be the destiny of nations and continents alike. There has never been a better time to pray than now. Let us pray!